What's It All About?

*Philosophy and the
Meaning of Life*

Julian Baggini

Granta Books
London

Granta Publications, 2/3 Hanover Yard, Noel Road, London N1 8BE

First published in Great Britain by Granta Books 2004
This edition published by Granta Books 2005

A CIP catalogue record for this book is available from the British Library.

3 5 7 9 10 8 6 4 2

Typeset by M Rules

Printed and bound in Great Britain by Bookmarque Limited, Croydon, Surrey

Acknowledgements

The two people who require thanking above all others are Lizzy Kremer and George Miller, without both of whom this book would not have seen the light of day, nor deserved to.

I can't bring myself to list the others I need to thank without pointing out a curious purpose the list of acknowledgements seems to have, especially in academic journals. Often it seems to be a means of signalling to the wider world how important and well connected the author is. There should always be at least two or three intellectual heavyweights in the list of people thanked, just to show the good company the author keeps.

Let me just say, then, that this list does not describe my social circle, but simply lists those who have responded to requests for information or otherwise helped me out, in ways great or small. They are Nicholas Fearn, Mathew Iredale, Oliver James, Jonathan Rée, John Shand, Jeremy Stangroom and Galen Strawson. Thanks also to Sajidah Ahmad, Gillian Kemp, Lesley Levene, Alison and David Worthington and Louise Campbell. If I've left anyone out, I'm very sorry. I have a feeling my memory isn't as good as it used to be, but to be honest, I can't remember how good it used to be.

Contents

Introduction

'You're T. S. Eliot,' said a taxi driver to the famous poet as he stepped into his cab. Eliot asked him how he knew. 'Ah, I've got an eye for a celebrity,' he replied. 'Only the other evening I picked up Bertrand Russell, and I said to him, "Well, Lord Russell, what's it all about?" And, do you know, he couldn't tell me.'

On which man is the joke in this true story? Is it Lord Russell, the great philosopher, who despite all his supposed intelligence and wisdom was unable to answer the cabby's question? Surely if anyone can tell us 'what it's all about', the world's greatest living philosopher can? Or is it the taxi driver, who expected to hear the solution to such a big problem in the course of a short journey? Even if Russell knew the answer, wouldn't it require time and patience to explain the secrets of the universe?

Perhaps the best answer is that neither man merits mockery. Certainly not Russell, for if it were possible to answer the question properly in ten minutes someone would already have publicly done so and the taxi driver would not have needed to ask. But nor should we mock the taxi driver for his ignorance. His question is one almost everyone asks at some point.

The problem is that it is vague, general and unclear. It is not so much a single question but a place-holder for a whole set of questions: Why are we here? What is the purpose of life? Is it enough just to be happy? Is my life serving some greater purpose? Are we here to help others or just ourselves?

What's it all about?

To answer these questions I believe we need to undertake a rational, secular inquiry. By 'secular' I do not mean 'atheist'. I mean simply that our arguments must not start from any supposed revealed truths, religious doctrines or sacred texts. Instead they must appeal to reasons, evidence and arguments that can be understood and assessed by all, whether they have a faith or not. This is because even for many believers, the authority of established religions cannot be taken as absolute. As we understand the great diversity of faiths in the world, the historical events and forces that shaped their doctrines and sacred texts, and the fallibility of many of their leaders, the idea that they provide direct access to absolute truth loses its credibility. Divinely inspired or not, the human hand is all too clearly present. That means that even if we do believe, we cannot accept religious teachings unquestioningly. We must use our own intelligence to determine for ourselves whether or not the answers they provide stand up. And because at some stage most of us can't help but wonder what it's all about, we can't avoid this kind of philosophizing for ever.

The subject may appear to be so difficult and deep that even to attempt to write a book on it is hubristic. That accusation could be made against me if I were claiming that the 'meaning of life' is a kind of secret that only the select few can discover through contemplation, revelation or a lifetime of intellectual inquiry. Such promises imply that the meaning of life is like a piece of knowledge that, once discovered, unlocks all the mysteries of life and explains everything. And because quite clearly the vast majority of us don't have any knowledge of this big secret, one needs to be especially wise to have uncovered it.

I think this whole idea is bogus and expect most readers would agree. If there were such a big secret, word would probably have got round by now. The whole problem of life's meaning is not that we lack any particular piece of secret information that would allow us to understand it; the question is not one that can be solved by any discovery of new evidence. It is rather to be solved by thinking about the issues on which the evidence remains silent. Much of what is to follow will, I hope, demonstrate this.

Hence I would describe the account of the meaning of life given in this book as 'deflationary', in that it reduces the mythical, single and mysterious question of 'the meaning of life' to a series of smaller and utterly unmysterious questions about various meanings in life. In this way it shows the question of the meaning of life to be at the same time something less and something more than it is usually taken to be: less because it is not a grand mystery beyond the reach of most of us; and more because it is not one question but many.

These questions can be answered, not because I possess exceptional wisdom, but simply by drawing together the wisdom of the greats of the past. In selecting and presenting their ideas, however, I am necessarily presenting a personal view and not just a dispassionate survey of what philosophers have to say. This is one person's account, albeit one with which I hope the majority of philosophers would mostly agree.

Anyone embarking on a quest to discover the meaning of life could do worse than heed the warning of Douglas Adams's *The Hitch Hiker's Guide to the Galaxy*. In this story, a race of beings fed up with bickering over the meaning of life decide to build a supercomputer to provide them with the answer. Deep Thought, as it is known, takes seven and a half million years to provide an answer to the question of 'life, the universe and everything'. On the day of reckoning, with 'infinite majesty and calm', Deep Thought finally gives its verdict: 'Forty-two.'

The trouble is that the designers of the computer demanded an answer to 'the question of life, the universe and everything' without bothering to ask whether they really knew what this question was. Now they have the answer, they don't understand it because they don't know what it is an answer to. Asking the right questions is as important as giving the right answers.

There will never be a last word on the meaning of life, partly because each individual has to satisfy herself that she has asked the right questions and found satisfactory answers. The search for meaning is essentially personal. This book cannot provide a map showing exactly where your search will end, if indeed it ever does. It can, however, provide some navigational aids to help with that search. How they are used, and how useful they are, are for you to judge.

1

Looking for the blueprint

For millions this life is a sad vale of tears
Sitting round with really nothing to say
While scientists say we're just simply spiralling coils
Of self-replicating DNA
MONTY PYTHON'S THE MEANING OF LIFE

Why are we here?

'Who was I? What was I? Whence did I come? What was my destination? These questions continually recurred, but I was unable to solve them.'

Any creature capable of conscious reflection will almost certainly ask questions like these at some point, often without being able to find satisfactory answers. The questioner in this instance, however, is in a rather unusual position. He is the creation of Victor Frankenstein in Mary Shelley's Gothic fable. And unlike humans, this creature was able to find out the truth about his origins and why he was created. Did that mean that he discovered the meaning of his own life? And might we discover the meanings of our lives by finding out more about our origins?

Frankenstein will reappear later. First, as I indicated in the introduction, to find the right answers we have to start with a clear understanding of the questions. 'What's it all about?' could be taken to mean 'Why are we here?' However, this question is ambiguous, inviting two very different kinds of response. One explains the *causes* of why we are here; it is past-orientated and about origins. The other explains the *purpose* of our existence; it is future-orientated and about destinations. In Aristotle's terminology, the first kind of explanation is about efficient causes, the second, final causes (although it does not involve any causation in the modern sense). So, for example, what goes on in the kitchen is the efficient cause of my dinner, and my eating it is the final cause.

Sometimes the two kinds of answer fit together. That is to say, the story of what caused something to exist is also the story of its future purpose. For example, the story of why a road was built is also the story of what its future purpose is: to allow cars to travel along it. However, the two answers need not be connected. Consider wild berries that are gathered for food by humans. The story of their origins – how they evolved – is not the story of what purpose they serve for humans who come along and eat them, unless we say that God created wild berries *so that* we could eat them. This is a kind of answer I would resist for reasons I will shortly explain. For the moment we simply need to note that we cannot assume that answering the question about something's origins tells us about its future or present purpose.

For this reason, in this chapter I'm going to focus on the question of the origins of human life and what, if anything, that can tell us about life's meaning. The question of future or present purpose will be the subject of the next chapter.

Corners of dots on specks on fragments

In some ways there isn't really any big mystery about the origins of human life. Rather there are two major competing clusters of theories, both of which leave many details unexplained, but which also provide enough of a framework for us to consider their implications for life's meaning. These two theories are creationism and naturalism.

Creationist theories claim that the originator of human life is some supernatural agency working with some conscious purpose in mind. Naturalist theories claim that human life emerged as part of a blind process that is not the product of any intelligent design. There are some hybrid positions, such as those that see the creator God as being an inextricable part of nature itself rather than a supernatural agency working outside it. But even these hybrids can be classified for our current purposes as either creationist or naturalist on the grounds of whether they see the origins of life as a result of intelligent purpose (creationism) or purposeless natural processes (naturalism).

Consider naturalism first. There is now a standard naturalist story about the origins of human life. Many details remain contentious but the broad framework is largely agreed upon by scientists. This story begins with the Big Bang fifteen billion years ago, continues with the formation of our sun ten billion years later, and comes up to date with the relatively recent emergence of primitive single-cell life forms, which through the process of evolution culminated – from our point of view – in the emergence of *Homo sapiens* a mere 600,000 years ago. When asked how God fits into this picture, scientists will usually echo the words of the French scientist Laplace, who responded to a similar question from Napoleon by saying, 'I have no need of that hypothesis.'

It is remarkable how well corroborated this story is, when you consider that the evidence for it comes from a number of disparate sciences, including cosmology, theoretical physics, astronomy, biology and biochemistry. The evidence that the naturalist account is broadly true is overwhelming. Nevertheless, my concern here is not to show that it is true, but to consider the implications for life's meaning *if* it is true. Many see these implications as profoundly disturbing.

The worry many people have is that if the naturalist account is true, then life can only be a meaningless accident of nature. If there is any meaning at all, then it only concerns the grander unfolding of the universe's destiny and human beings are irrelevant. As Bertrand Russell put it, 'The universe may have a purpose, but nothing we know suggests that, if so, this purpose has any similarity to ours.'

Consider, for example, the account of human evolution presented in Richard Dawkins's *The Selfish Gene*. According to Dawkins, natural selection takes place at the level of the gene rather than at the level of the whole organism or species. This means that individual organisms, including human beings, are in his words 'survival machines', built according to the instructions encoded in DNA, and with the 'purpose' of ensuring the survival of the gene, not the organism itself. From a biological point of view, then, the life of an individual human is not of prime importance. What matters is that the genes carried by the human are passed on and survive.

I needed to put 'purpose' in scare-quotes because we cannot attribute purposes to genes or organisms in the usual sense. This is because genes are not designed to fulfil any purpose, nor do they have desires or goals, conscious or otherwise. Genes simply survive if they have effects, first on the organisms that carry them and second on the wider environment, which are conducive to their survival. But because those that do survive by definition have the characteristics suitable to ensure their survival, there is an appearance or illusion that these characteristics serve the purpose of ensuring their survival. But these purposes are not designed or given in advance, just as Dawkins does not believe that the eponymous 'selfish' genes are literally self-centred and egotistical.

Where does this leave individual human beings, or even the species *Homo sapiens*? At best, if we do serve a purpose, that purpose is to continue the existence of our genes. At worst, we can't talk about purpose or meaning at all, since the process of random mutation and replication has no purpose and no goal as its end. As the Monty Python song goes, 'we're just simply spiralling coils of self-replicating DNA.'

The naturalist story as a whole provokes similar reactions. To quote Russell again,

'In the visible world, the Milky Way is a tiny fragment; within this fragment, the solar system is an infinitesimal speck, and of the speck our planet is a microscopic dot. On this dot, tiny lumps of impure carbon and water, of complicated structure, with somewhat unusual physical and chemical qualities, crawl about for a few years, until they are dissolved again into the elements of which they are compounded.'

Seen from this vantage point, human life is a purposeless, insignificant accident.

Sartre's paper-knife

This is the conclusion often associated with the late-nineteenth- and early-twentieth-century existentialist philosophers. A superficial reading of their key texts might support this interpretation. Friedrich Nietzsche described himself as 'the first perfect nihilist of Europe'; Albert Camus's most famous idea is that life is 'absurd'; and Jean-Paul Sartre talked about 'anguish, abandonment and despair'. With the supernatural removed from the world-view of modernity, all meaning has been ripped out of the universe and life is left without purpose.

However, even if we confine ourselves to existentialism's canonical texts, the full picture is not as bleak as these stark soundbites might suggest. Consider, for example, Sartre's *Existentialism and Humanism*, originally delivered as a public lecture to explain the basic tenets of existentialism. In it, Sartre does indeed talk of anguish, abandonment and despair; but he also claims that 'existentialism is optimistic'. Uncharitable readers may see this as evidence of Sartre's incoherence, but more sensitive interpreters will see it as a warning against taking some of the more strident of existentialism's slogans at face value.

It can be misleading to generalize too much about what 'existentialists' have to say about life's meaning, since those thinkers labelled as existentialist differed enormously in their beliefs. Most strikingly, although many of the best-known existentialists were atheists – including Sartre, Nietzsche and Camus – there were also religious existentialists, including Søren Kierkegaard, Gabriel Marcel and Karl Barth.

Nonetheless, the atheist existentialists do have something in common which relates importantly to our discussion of naturalism. All would agree that the 'discovery' that there is no God has created a crisis of meaning for human life. The reason for this is that we assumed that purpose and morality had their source in something outside of ourselves. When this assumption was overturned, we lost the source of life's meaning.

Sartre explains this with the analogy of a paper-knife. A paper-knife has a determinate 'essence' by virtue of the fact that it was created by someone to fulfil a certain function. In contrast, a sharp object like a flint has no essence, even though it too could be used to cut paper. It *just so happens* that humans have found a use for it.

Sartre's point is that we have assumed ourselves to be like paper-knives, not like pieces of flint. We believed that we had some kind of essential nature because God created us with a particular purpose in mind. But if God does not exist and the naturalist story is true, this picture is false. We are like the pieces of flint that just *are*. We may find uses for ourselves and others, but these purposes do not derive from our essential nature. And if naturalism is true, this observation holds for the entire universe and everything in it.

There are at least two ways of responding to this apparently bleak picture. One is simply to accept that life is therefore meaningless. The other is to question the assumption underpinning the pessimistic conclusion: that we need to be like paper-knives for life to have meaning. The crisis in meaning which the atheist existentialists identified is the result of our coming to realize that what we assumed to be true of human beings – that their purpose was given to them by their creator – is actually false. Far from leaving life meaningless, this may simply lead us to conclude that the source of life's meaning is not where we thought.

This is roughly the direction in which Sartre's thought goes. For Sartre, the crucial truth we have to recognize is that because purpose and meaning are not built in to human life, we ourselves are responsible for fashioning our own purposes. It is not that life has no meaning, but that it has no *predetermined* meaning. This requires us to confront our own responsibility for creating meaning for ourselves, something which Sartre believes we would much rather not do. We would prefer to live our lives in 'bad faith', pretending that how we live and ought to live are not down to our choice but a product of fate, outside forces or supernatural design.

The idea that our destinies are in a sense in our own hands, that we are free to create our own purposes, can sound empowering and liberating. For many, however, it rings hollow. It is as though we confront the reality of a meaningless universe by saying we're just going to make meaning up for ourselves. But a made-up meaning is no real meaning at all. Sartrean purpose is pretend purpose, existentialist values are counterfeit values.

There are, however, reasons for believing this response is misguided. Why should we think that assigned purposes are inferior to predetermined purposes, and that only the latter can make life meaningful? There is no general principle that purposes are more 'real' or important if they are introduced at the design stage. Consider the history of the Post-it note. The repositionable adhesive that the notes use was discovered by a scientist working for 3M in 1968. However, neither he nor anyone else in the company had any idea what possible use such an adhesive could be put to. Six years later, another 3M scientist, tired of losing his place in the hymnal while singing in his church choir, thought how useful a lightly adhesive bookmark would be. He then realized that the apparently useless glue was useful after all. Now Post-it notes are ubiquitous.

The Post-it note may seem like a trivial example, but it illustrates neatly the point that, when it comes to use or purpose, what matters is not necessarily what the inventor had in mind, but the uses or purposes the innovation actually has.

Human life may be a very different context, but the same logic applies. What matters is surely that life has a purpose for us, here and now. Whether this purpose was dreamed up by a creator or is assigned or invented by ourselves is not of paramount importance. If we can give life purpose and meaning, there is no obvious reason why this should be considered an inferior kind of meaning to that which could have been given by a creator.

Indeed, predetermined purposes could conceivably make life less meaningful. Consider, for example, the case of a latter-day Frankenstein who might create a human being for the sole purpose of cleaning his house. Surely this life would have less dignity and meaning than the life of a person born into a naturalistic universe? It would be better for this creature to determine its own purposes than simply to fulfil the desires of its creator.

This is one reason why Sartre thought his existentialism was optimistic. Because human beings have the power to determine their own purposes, they have greater potential for leading meaningful lives than mere artefacts that are assigned an essence by their creators. For the ability to choose one's own purposes is part of what distinguishes what Sartre calls a conscious 'being-for-itself' from an unconscious 'being-in-itself'. The being-for-itself can take control of its own life and use its conscious thought to direct its own purposes, whereas the being-in-itself can only be what it is and what others use it for.

Where does this leave the problem of meaning in a naturalist universe? If we take the naturalist view that the universe is the product not of intelligent design but of natural forces, then the explanation of why we are here does not bring with it any answer to the question of what purpose our lives may hold. This may appear to lead to a form of nihilism, in which we see the universe as devoid of meaning. But this conclusion only follows if we make the false assumption that purpose has to come built in to human life.

The fact, then, that we can find no purpose or meaning in the origins of human life is no reason for supposing human life *has* no purpose or meaning.

Although many of these ideas were first clearly articulated by the existentialists, philosophers of many different stripes agree with their basic claims. Daniel C. Dennett, for example, a contemporary American philosopher no one would describe as an existentialist, writes, 'Why should our purposes have to be inherited from on high? (I call that the trickle-down theory of importance – everything important has to get its importance from something else that is even more important.) Why can't we invent our own purposes?'

This case should seem to strengthen as this book progresses, for we will be looking at other ways in which life can be said to be meaningful, as well as returning to the theme that ultimately human life is itself the source of its own meaning. But first we must consider the alternative to the naturalist view: that life's origin and meaning are explained by intelligent design.

Adam's puzzling purpose

For most of human history, and even today, most people have not accepted the naturalist view that the universe is the product of blind, purposeless forces. They think that the universe must have some kind of creator, usually called God.

This belief is vividly expressed in the various creation stories of the world's religions. Jews and Christians have the stories of Genesis, in which God created the world in six days. Hinduism has the Puranas, which tell a different tale, one that involves Lord Vishnu lying on his serpent, Shesha, and a lotus growing out of his navel, from which emerges Brahma, who then creates the entire universe in a little golden egg. Though many people view these as myths, it has to be remembered that many others believe them to be literally true.

Still other people reject these myths as literal truth but do believe that God is the ultimate cause of the universe: that the stories of Genesis and the Puranas are only metaphors, but reflect the truth that the universe was created deliberately and for a purpose. The idea that there must be some kind of cosmic designer is sometimes justified by sophisticated arguments but is perhaps more commonly supported by a kind of gut instinct, a strong compulsion many feel to believe that the universe can't be just a brute fact.

For example, the last man to walk on the moon, Eugene Cernan, said, 'No one in their right mind can look in the stars and the eternal blackness everywhere and deny the spirituality of the experience, nor the existence of a Supreme Being.' However, assertions like this are no more than expressions of personal conviction. When Cernan jumps from claims about the nature of his own internal, 'spiritual' experience to external facts about the existence of a creator, he does not provide any arguments or reasons for others to believe as he does. He merely maintains that everyone in his or her right mind will believe with the same certainty as him.

As with naturalism, my prime concern here is not to assess the merits of the various creationist views but to examine what accepting them would mean for our views about life's meaning and purpose. However, I should declare that I am not an impartial observer. I think that the creation stories of religious texts are obviously false in that they conflict with each other and our best scientific understanding of how the universe began. And along with the vast majority of contemporary philosophers, I am unpersuaded by versions of the so-called cosmological and teleological arguments in philosophy that attempt to demonstrate that God must be the first cause or designer of the universe.

But assume that I am wrong and that creationism is true. As we saw in the previous section, people are quick to conclude that if there is no creator God then there is no meaning or purpose to life. Yet it is not clear how *with* a creator God there *is* meaning or purpose. All that seems to follow from a belief that the universe was created is that the designer has some purpose in mind for us. What that purpose is and whether we should welcome it are left undetermined.

This is not intended as a criticism or argument against religion, but a simple fact about the limitations of religious explanation which believers too should (and often do) accept. No Christian or Jew, for example, can provide an adequate answer to the question of why God created us by referring to their sacred texts. All we are told in Genesis is that God told man to 'Be fruitful and increase in number; fill the earth and subdue it. Rule over the fish of the sea and the birds of the air and over every living creature that moves on the ground' (Genesis 1:28).

Indeed, as the account progresses, even more mundane claims for the purpose of humanity are made. 'The Lord God took the man and put him in the Garden of Eden to work it and take care of it,' it says (2:15), and Eve was created because 'no suitable helper was found' (2:20). Many interpret this as indicating that we have been given custodianship of the planet. But we don't have any idea why it needs looking after in the first place or how doing this job can give our lives meaning.

Of course, no Christian or Jew who holds these texts to be sacred would claim that they exhaust all there is to say about why

God created us. But other religious explanations don't provide adequate accounts either. For instance, it is often said that we are here to do God's will. If this were true we would be like the house-cleaning monster described earlier. Our lives would have a purpose for the being that created us but not a purpose for us. We would each be like Sartre's being-in-itself – an object to be used for the ends of others – and not a being-for-itself – a conscious being making choices meaningful for itself. If we found that our sole purpose was to serve God then we might think that was a worse fate than to have no predetermined purpose at all. Is it better to be slaves with a role in the universe or to be free people left to create a role for ourselves?

This view that we are created to serve God is not only objectionable on the grounds that it robs humanity of its dignity. It also has to be seen as extremely implausible within the world-view of the religions that sometimes propound it. After all, what could seem more unlikely than that the supreme being would feel the need to create human beings, with all their complexity, and with all the suffering and toil that human life entails, solely so that it can have creatures to serve it? This is an image of God as an egotistical tyrant, determined to use its power to surround itself with acolytes and have praise heaped upon it. This is not the God which most religious believers worship, and so the idea that we are here just to serve such a God is not one that should be seriously countenanced either.

A more plausible answer can be traced back to Jesus' words in the Gospels: 'I have come that they may have life, and have it to the full' (John 10:10). That's a better answer even if it is not a particularly enlightening one. For one thing, an atheist can agree with it. Atheists too think that we should live life to the full, not because that is God's purpose but because this is the only life we've got and so we ought to make the most of it. In a sense, the sentiment expressed is just a platitude: who could think humans should not have life, and have it to the full?

Furthermore it doesn't tell us what makes one life fuller than another. Many religious believers will say that is what their sacred texts are for: follow the advice within and you will live life more fully. But it is significant that only fundamentalists follow this rule with any rigour. Most religious believers use their own judgement. They follow the rules set out in their sacred texts only if they think these promote a better life for all. Where they don't, the passages are mercifully ignored. For example, not many people believe that 'when any man reviles his father and his mother, he shall be put to death' (Leviticus 20:9) or that 'you may also buy the children of those who have settled and lodge with you . . . [and] may use them as slaves permanently' (25:45–46).

This is, I think, sensible. But it means that religious believers are following a simple rule: do what the sacred texts tell you to do if it promotes a better life for all and ignore it if it doesn't. But then this is the equivalent of an even simpler rule: do whatever promotes a better life for all. The sacred texts no longer have any particular authority and the rule to be followed is one that non-believers can embrace too. So the idea that our purpose in this life is to live full lives does not need to be rooted in any God-given instructions.

For this answer to have any particular religious content, it needs to be connected with the idea of an afterlife. If a full life includes life after death, then atheist and religious conceptions do part company. I'm going to set this question to one side for now, since I discuss the possibility of life after death in Chapter 3. What we should note for now is that only a belief in the afterlife seems to make the idea that God's purpose for us is to live full lives distinctive from the banal claim that life is to be lived.

I think that most reflective religious believers would agree that saying God's purpose for us is to serve it or live full lives is not adequate. They might prefer to say that the existence of God shows that there must be a purpose, since God wouldn't have created us without one, but that we do not know what that purpose is. Faith requires us to trust God and its purposes for us. As Jesus is reported in John's Gospel to have said, 'Trust in God; trust also in me. In my Father's house are many rooms' (14:1–2). This is a perfectly coherent position and probably the one most sensible religious believers occupy. But doing so requires an honest acceptance that they have no more idea as to what the purpose of life is than the atheist has.

The leap of faith required to adopt such a position also needs to be clearly understood. This is faith that a God we cannot know to exist has a purpose we cannot discern for an afterlife we have no evidence is to come. Further, we would also be trusting that this purpose is one we would be pleased with. If it turned out that our purpose was to fight Satan's hordes for eternity or just to have lived as a beacon of fortitude under duress on earth before dying, we might not be too pleased that God had a purpose for us after all.

A belief that we were created by God for a purpose does not then provide us with the kind of adequate account of life's meaning we might expect. Religions are not clear about what this purpose is. The idea that it is to serve God seems deeply implausible and contrary to most conceptions of God's nature. The idea that it is to live life to the full is a platitude, only turned into something more by a belief in an afterlife. The idea that God's purpose is something we just have to trust is an admission that we have no answer to the question of why we are here and must leave everything to the unknown. Believing that our origins are with a supernatural being does not, then, provide us with an explanation of what the meaning or purpose of life is. At best it merely reassures us that there is one.

Santa Claus and Frankenstein

Perhaps we should not be surprised that a consideration of why we are here, couched in terms of what explains our origins, has not been more enlightening. Consider again the case of Frankenstein's creature. Unlike us, he was actually able to discover why he was made and for what purpose. He chanced upon the journal Frankenstein kept in the four months leading to his creation. His initial reaction to reading it was rage and despair. 'Accursed creator!' he screamed. 'Why did you form a monster so hideous that even *you* turned from me in disgust?'

But these revelations did not have any significant lasting effect on the creature's journey through life and his quest for meaning. In many ways, he was in the same position after he discovered the truth about his origins as he was before: he was still an outcast, feared by humans yet longing for their company and affection. Nothing in the revelations about his creation helped or hindered him in his struggle to cope with these facts. In the end, what he decided would make his life at least tolerable was a female companion, and this he ordered Frankenstein to create.

Shelley was right to show that knowledge of the creature's origins did not reveal his life's meaning, for there is no reason why looking to the past will inform us about our present state and future prospects. The idea that it does is known as the 'genetic fallacy'. This term was coined by two philosophers, Morris Cohen and Ernest Nagel. The mistake they identified was of confusing the origins of a belief with its justification. Since then, the expression has come to be used more loosely to describe any kind of confusion between an account of origins and an account of something's current or future nature.

An obvious example of this fallacy is to think that the etymology of a word always provides a vital insight into how it is now used. For instance, consider the origin of the word 'digit'. It derives from the Latin *dicere*, which means to tell, say or point out. This gave rise to the meaning of a finger or thumb; and because these were used for counting, it also came to mean a numerical figure. This is all very interesting, but if you want to know what is meant when someone talks about a 'three-digit figure' your understanding is not best helped by considering the origins of the word 'digit'. Indeed, if you think too much about origins you might be misled.

It is also possible to pay too much attention to origins in other areas. For example, what if the urban myth were true and Santa Claus's coat was usually green until Coca-Cola's advertising campaigns in the 1930s dressed him in their corporate colours of red and white? Would that mean that all Santas today were subliminal advertisements for Coca-Cola? Some anti-capitalists might have you think so, but the claim would not be credible. The campaign would explain why Santa's coat came to be red, but it wouldn't explain how the image of Santa functions today.

When we think about the origins and purpose of life, a similar kind of genetic fallacy can be committed. The mistake is to think that understanding the origins of life automatically tells us its end goal or present purpose. But the one does not necessarily follow from the other. A piece of flint or an adhesive which came into being with no purpose at all can later be given purpose by a human who uses it. A building that was created with a specific purpose, such as a tollbooth, can become purposeless if the road is made into a free one. An original purpose or lack of purpose does not necessarily fix the purpose of the object for eternity. Purposes can be gained, lost or changed. That is why a consideration of life's origins has not enabled us to come up with any clear answer as to what life's purpose is, and why the naturalist belief that life was not created for a purpose does not mean that life can have no purpose.

Where else, then, can we look? As I said at the beginning of this chapter, the question 'Why are we here?' can have two interpretations. One looks back to our origins. The other looks at our future goals. That is the subject of the next chapter.

2

Living life forwards

Life can only be understood backwards; but it must be lived forwards.
SØREN KIERKEGAARD, *JOURNALS*

Order in the chaos

The Wild West portrayed in the films of Sergio Leone is like the
state of nature described by the seventeenth-century political
philosopher Thomas Hobbes. With only weak sheriffs to uphold
the law, there is a constant 'war of all against all' and so life is
'solitary, poor, nasty, brutish and short'. It is like the kind of amoral,
anarchic world that many fear is an inevitable consequence of the
death of God and the loss of absolute values that comes with it.

Yet there is the possibility of some kind of order and meaning
even in this moral vacuum. In *For a Few Dollars More*, for example, the
two main protagonists at first appear to be archetypes of amorality:
bounty hunters. It transpires, however, that one of them, the
Colonel (played by Lee Van Cleef), is driven by a greater purpose
than simply wealth. He is on a lifelong mission to avenge the rape
and murder of his sister by finding the man who did it and
confronting him with the memory of his crime before killing him.

The same revenge theme is played out in *Once Upon a Time in the West*. This time a man with no name, played by Charles Bronson, seeks to avenge the murder of his brother and make the murderer know why he is about to die.

The objectives that drive the protagonists do not just give shape to the films' narratives. They show how a sense of purpose can give shape and meaning to lives even in a world filled with meaningless death and struggle. They reflect the desire we often feel for a clear future purpose that will make our own struggles meaningful and give our lives a clear direction.

A perceived lack of such a purpose is often at the root of much unease about the value of life. Many people believe that the world would not notice if they were gone, that nothing they do is of any significance. Life is taken up by earning money, eating, drinking and sleeping, punctuated by periods of rest and relaxation, all activities that have no further purpose other than keeping us alive and sane. It is tempting to think that if only our deeds could have a higher purpose or goal, then our lives would be meaningful.

What we seem to be looking for here is a 'teleological' account of human life: an explanation given in terms of future goals or objectives. The classic account of teleology and the human good is found in Aristotle's *Nicomachean Ethics*. Aristotle's great insight was that teleological explanations, in order to be complete, must terminate with something which is an end in itself. One can see why by simply considering how one responds to a curious and insistent child.

As many parents will know, most children go through a 'why phase' of varying length and intensity. They demand to know why they must do anything or why anything happens at all. It is for this reason that Isaiah Berlin reputedly described philosophers as adults who persist in asking childish questions. The problem for both parent and child is that the child does not know when to stop and the parent often does not know how to stop them.

Consider one such trying conversation:

- Why are there so many cars on the street?
- Because people have to get to work and take their children to school.
- Why do people have to go to work?
- Because they need to earn money.
- Why do they need to earn money?
- So they can afford to live in nice houses and eat well.
- Why can't they just live in huts and eat like they used to in the olden days?
- Because that isn't as nice as living in a comfortable house.
- Why not?
- *It just isn't!* Look! It's the ice-cream man!

The possibility of such a conversation being endless is inherent in its very structure. For any statement 'A' it is possible to ask 'Why A?' This will yield the answer 'because B'. But then, of course, it is always possible to ask 'Why B?' and so on, ad infinitum. The only way to end this potentially endless series is to draw the exchange to a halt arbitrarily, as the parent does, or come up with an answer, 'because X', for which the question 'Why X?' is unnecessary, misguided or nonsensical. We can often do this for activities where the context is understood and taken for granted.

For example, if you are playing chess and I ask you why you moved your rook, you might reply by saying that you are preparing to checkmate in three moves. In the context of chess it is clearly misguided for me to ask why you would want to do that. But if I am interested in why you are even bothering to live, the question becomes meaningful again. I might well wonder why you want to win your game, because I might want to know why you think playing chess forms part of a meaningful life.

The problem is that when it comes to life's overall purpose, such answers are hard to find. Can this difficulty be resolved?

Time for justifications

A possible way out is provided by the logical structure of the dilemma. The 'why/because' series is essentially a sequence of justifications. It is easy to assume that this must correspond to a sequence in time. So, for example, when we considered the origins of life in the previous chapter we were essentially examining a 'why/because' series which stretched back from the present to the past. We asked why we were born, then why our parents were born, back to why there are humans at all and ended up at the Big Bang or the myths of Genesis. That series terminated without revealing life's meaning.

In this chapter we have turned our attention to the future, and so it is tempting to think that the 'why/because' series will have to extend into the future until such time as we can stop it. However, a 'why/because' series need not be temporal. For example, consider everyone's role in a restaurant. If we ask why the waiters, cooks, dishwashers, maître d', diners and so on all do what they do, the explanations will not essentially be given in terms of future goals or past events. Rather everyone is fulfilling a mutually supportive role where the activities of one meet the needs of or supply purposes for the other. Our 'why' questions invite 'because' answers that explain things simultaneously, as well as with regard to past or future.

Even when a 'why/because' series has a temporal dimension, it need not follow one direction in time only. Consider this example:

- Why are you driving to Doncaster?
- Because I'm taking my uncle's ashes to where he wants them to be scattered. (Future)
- Why are you doing that?
- Because I promised him I would. (Past)
- But he's dead, so why do you feel the need to honour that promise? He'll never know.
- Because it's important to me that I'm the kind of person who keeps his word. (Present)
- Why?
- . . .

In this example, aspects of the past, present and future are all used as part of the 'why/because' series of justifications. This shows how it is far too limiting to see 'why/because' series as having to trail off either into the past or into the future.

This is an important point. I have rejected the view that life's purpose can be understood by looking backwards to its origins. But that doesn't mean the only alternative is looking forward to its ultimate end. Just as the restaurant staff are fulfilling their professional purposes in the present simply by doing their job, couldn't we fulfil life's purpose in the present simply by living our lives? I am going to argue that something like this must be true. But first we need to consider a little further the possibility that the future will provide us with meaning.

Can I die now?

If we see life's purpose as the achievement of future goals, several problems arise. If we are mortal, the problem is simply that there will come a time when we have no future. Life would end with meaning unfulfilled, since death would eventually rob us of the future where the purposes for our actions lie.

For the same reason, even if we were immortal this would not provide life with a purpose. Indeed, it could make life seem even more futile. We would be condemned to live a life where the only answers to questions of why we do anything belong in the eternal future. We would be like donkeys wearing hats from which carrots are suspended two feet in front of our eyes, forever moving forward in time towards a forever unachievable future.

So if life is to be meaningful, the 'why/because' series cannot extend indefinitely into the future. At some point we have to reach an end point where a further 'why' question is unnecessary, misguided or nonsensical. Otherwise the purpose of life is forever beyond our reach.

These insights are reflected in Sergio Leone's Westerns. There is a completeness and closure at the end of the films because the goals of the protagonists have finally been achieved. Their objectives do not lie in the eternal future, but in a future which one day becomes the present, and in turn the past.

But this gives rise to a further problem. As the credits roll and the hero rides off into the desert, the question the films do not confront is what gives the gunslinger his purpose in life *now*. When people fulfil a lifetime's ambition they often jokingly say, 'I can die happy.' But this invites the serious reply, 'Why not?' After all, if life is about the achievement of a goal, then once that goal is reached, what is there left to do? Once life's purpose has been fulfilled, it no longer guides our actions, apparently leaving us with nothing to live for.

This is not just intellectual sophistry. Many goal-orientated people do feel this way once they have achieved their ambitions. Initial elation provides a temporary glow, but soon they are left with a kind of emptiness as they realize that, now all they have been working for has been accomplished, they have nothing left to give purpose to their life.

A good example of this (originally from Alfie Kohn's *No Contest*) is cited by the contemporary Australian moral philosopher Peter Singer in his *How Are We to Live?* The coach of the Dallas Cowboys, Tom Landry, said, 'Even after you've just won the Super Bowl – *especially* after you've just won the Super Bowl – *there's always next year*. If "winning isn't everything. It's the only thing" then "the only thing" is nothing – emptiness, the nightmare of life without meaning.'

This illustrates how if the meaning of life is tied to goal-achievement, then achieving that goal can leave you with 'emptiness' – nothing left to provide meaning. The way many people try to get around this is simply to set another goal – '*there's always next year*'. But this simply avoids confronting the fundamental flaw in seeing life in this way. As the Danish existentialist Søren Kierkegaard said, life 'must be lived forwards', in a present that constantly transforms the future into the past. Moments in time cannot be kept hold of, yet achievements are of their essence tied to moments of success, which all too quickly drift into the past.

This reflects a tension in the human condition captured by Kierkegaard's distinction between what he called the aesthetic and ethical spheres of existence. Each sphere reflects an important aspect of human life, but neither by itself is sufficient to fully explain it. A neat illustration of this is provided by Patrice Leconte's film *L'Homme du train*. The two protagonists envy each other, and we can understand why by seeing how they have lived their lives too much on one side of Kierkegaard's aesthetic/ethical divide. The retired schoolteacher, Manesquier, has lived a quiet life, one which has been attached to things of 'eternal' value which belong to the ethical sphere: education, learning, art and poetry. Such a life does justice to our nature as beings that persist over time, with memories and plans as well as present sensations. It reflects the fact that we do not live just in the moment but over continuous and connected periods of time.

But there is more to life than the ethical, as Manesquier comes to realize. He yearns for some of the intense experiences that his new friend, Milan, a serial robber, has had. Milan has lived life in the aesthetic sphere, devoted to the present moment. 'Aesthetic' in this context is used not with its present-day associations with art and beauty, but with its original Greek meaning, as pertaining to sensory experience. We are aesthetic beings in that we experience the world through our senses, in the here and now. Milan's life recognizes this fact, but he is left weary and empty by his series of escapades, none of which has provided enduring satisfaction. He sees in Manesquier's life precisely what his life has been missing. This supports Kierkegaard's claim that a life which is lived only in the present is inherently unsatisfactory, for the very reason that the moment always eludes us. The present cannot be grasped: it always melts through our fingers and becomes the past.

Milan and Manesquier represent the duality of human life, its sometimes conflicting needs; and their contrasting dissatisfactions highlight the need to live with due respect to both the aesthetic and the ethical.

Kierkegaard thought that the ethical and the aesthetic could not be rationally reconciled. He ridiculed Hegel's view that opposites –

thesis and antithesis – can always be resolved by the rational process of 'dialectic' into a harmonious 'synthesis'. Kierkegaard argued that only a leap of faith into the religious sphere could bring together these two conflicting aspects of human existence. In Christ, Kierkegaard saw the aesthetic and the ethical reconciled: finite man and infinite God coexisting in the figure of Jesus, not as something that can be rationally explained but as something that can only be embraced by going beyond rationality and into the realm of faith.

There are many reasons why Kierkegaard's analysis of the problem is more appealing than his solution. Kierkegaard's whole point is that there is no rational reason why one should make this leap of faith: the motivation to do so can only come from a prior commitment. Indeed, Kierkegaard himself saw his whole intellectual project as addressing the question of how he could become a true Christian. So unless we already have Christian faith, there is no good reason, even by Kierkegaard's own lights, to adopt that faith ourselves. For any inquiry that starts with no prior religious commitments, such as this one, embracing the contradiction of God made man has no great merits.

Nevertheless, Kierkegaard's analysis of the human condition can illuminate the problem of the goal-orientated life. The difficulty such a life faces is that it locates the purpose of life in the achievement of the goal, which is necessarily tied to a discrete moment in time. This reflects the aesthetic nature of human life. We are tied to the present and we must expect some of life's meaning to reflect that. But we also exist across time, and when our life's goals are fixed so narrowly on moments that are only briefly the present, we fail to do justice to the enduring aspect of human life.

La dolce vita

If the goal-orientated life is too rooted in the aesthetic, one obvious way to rectify the imbalance is to strive for desirable states of affairs as well as events. Consider the example of someone who thinks that once she has a large house in the south of France with a husband and children, then the 'why/because' series will have ended. This may sound shallow, but it is plausible. Consider this somewhat simplified version of how she might describe her life's goals.

- Why did you go to university?
- To get a degree so I could get a well-paid job.
- Why did you want a well-paid job?
- Because I wanted to earn lots of money.
- But that took hard work. Why was that more important than enjoying yourself?
- Well, it wasn't all hard work, and in any case, I was taking the longer view.
- Why?
- Because it enabled me to get where I am now: I have a huge house in the south of France with a swimming pool, a loving husband and wonderful children.
- Why would you want that?
- Are you nuts? Why wouldn't anyone want that?

The final 'why' question, although not nonsensical, could be seen as unnecessary or misguided. Hasn't the questioner just missed something if he thinks this idyllic life stands in need of some justification? We might question the morality of such a life in a world where so many go without basic necessities, but it does seem odd to question its desirability. After all, if this kind of life isn't worth living, which is?

The point here isn't to justify this particular lifestyle but to draw our attention to two important considerations. The first is that, as we have repeatedly seen, at some point we have to reach the stage where a 'why' question can be met with an answer along the lines of 'Are you nuts? Why wouldn't anyone want that?' If not, the 'why/because' series just extends into the indefinite future. And it does seem more satisfactory to end the series with a sustainable state of affairs than an event which then itself quickly passes into history.

The second point is even more telling. In justifying her life choices, this woman rests her case entirely on the final outcome: her wealth and family in later life. So the life-plan this woman has followed is premised on the possibility that the purpose of human life can be, not a particular achievement, but a desirable and sustainable state of affairs or lifestyle.

Once we accept that this is true, it should be evident that the kind of lifestyle it takes years of hard work and the accumulation of wealth to enjoy is but one of the possible kinds of lifestyles which are desirable in themselves. Yet so many of us do look towards some idyllic future when we have 'made it' as providing purpose for what we do. This is a mistake and at its root is a failure to realize that if what is being worked towards is worthwhile in itself, then so are many other things that are within our grasp right now. After all, the difference between the luxury lifestyle described and a moderately affluent one is only a matter of degree. For most of us, life isn't improved that much because the music is being played on a better hi-fi, or because the car being driven is a Jaguar rather than a Ford.

The person who sacrifices too much enjoyment of life to serve the purpose of future wealth and security is thus making the mistake of overestimating the extent to which his future life will be better than the one he could have now. Being wealthy may make life a bit better but not so much better that it is worth sacrificing years of one's life to work for. This is even more important when it comes to personal relationships, which are consistently highlighted by psychologists as being important for personal happiness. Neglecting friendships for work is almost inevitably a poor trade-off in terms of life satisfaction, since they are precisely the kind of thing which cannot simply be bought once one has become sufficiently wealthy. How many marriages and partnerships have been put under strain or even ruined by one partner spending so much time at work that they neglect their relationship?

The risk is not only that the future won't be good enough to justify the past, but also that the future will never come. For one of the great risks of making life's purpose some future goal is that, as mortal creatures, we can never be sure we will live to see that day. Most of us can hope to live to seventy or more years. But to *assume* we will do so is to take for granted that which can only be hoped for.

Of course, when balancing considerations of future and present there is no simple either/or. Many entrepreneurs, for example, love the process of making money itself and are not simply driven by the thought of the lifestyle they will be able to enjoy in the future. Indeed, it is a feature of most entrepreneurs that they don't stop working hard, even when they have long ceased needing to earn more money.

Nevertheless, whether it is wealth or some other future achievement we seek, it is tempting to think that satisfaction in life depends on things that are yet to come. Just as soon as the kids have left home, the mortgage has been paid off, I've climbed the promotion ladder and won't have to work quite so hard. Then life will be good. Philip Larkin captures this brilliantly in his poem 'Next, Please':

> *Always too eager for the future, we*
> *Pick up bad habits of expectancy.*
> *Something is always approaching; every day*
> *Till then we say . . .*

This 'till then' way of thinking stands between us and getting the kind of satisfaction available from life right now.

Perhaps one reason why we fall prey to 'till then' thinking is a form of bad faith, whereby we refuse to accept that something lies within our own control and responsibility and think that it depends on external factors, such as our financial situation. But although it is true that financial strain has a negative impact on personal happiness, whether or not we feel under strain because of our finances depends, unless we are very poorly off, largely on how we perceive things. As the Roman Stoic philosopher and emperor Marcus Aurelius said, albeit with a dash of overstatement, 'If you are distressed by any external thing, it is not this thing which disturbs you, but your own judgement about it. And it is in your power to wipe out that judgement now.'

Modern psychology echoes this sentiment. As the psychologist Oliver James has repeatedly pointed out, we are more miserable if we compare our financial situation with those better off than ourselves, and yet people tend to do just that, ignoring all those people who are as well off as or worse off than themselves.

Perceiving a comparative disadvantage, people then become less satisfied.

This kind of invidious comparison can go to ludicrous extremes and is satirized in Bret Easton Ellis's novel *American Psycho*. In the film adaptation, the protagonist, Patrick Bateman, is so infuriated that a Wall Street colleague has a better business card than his already excessively luxurious one that he becomes homicidal. The idea that someone is better off than him is just unbearable, even though he is obscenely well off in any case. The comparisons we tend to make are not usually as ridiculous as this, but if the content of the judgement is extraordinary, its form is most certainly not.

To acknowledge the central importance of our own responses, however, requires us to accept that it is within our own power to ease our dissatisfaction. Sartre claims that this kind of freedom is something we fear and try to deny. We don't like to think that it is all down to us, for if it is we have no one to blame if things go wrong. So we prefer instead to think, in bad faith, that it is not us but circumstances that are to blame.

Another reason why we might prefer to think we will be happy only when all the external factors are in place is that we find it hard to accept the imperfections of life. Sartre again has a word for this. He describes the need to accept the *facticity* of existence: the way the world is whether we like it or not.

This is very significant when it comes to what we desire and expect from life. What people in the affluent west typically want is a great partner who is both a terrific friend and a terrific lover; a good material standard of living; well-adjusted, happy children; a stimulating and fulfilling job; a varied social life with interesting, amusing and intelligent friends; and regular holidays abroad. Of course, one only needs to read the list to realize that very few people have all these things. Yet there is a widespread belief among the western middle classes, sometimes verging on the expectation, that all this can and should be achieved almost by right.

For example, author and journalist Hope Edelman would seem to have everything going for her: a good partner, a great job and a healthy child. But when her husband suggested they hired a nanny, she was horrified. 'Didn't he understand?' she explained. 'My plan hadn't been to hire someone to raise our child. My plan had been to do it together: two responsible parents with two fulfilling jobs, in an egalitarian marriage with a well-adjusted kid who was equally bonded to us both.' Such unrealistically high expectations are not uncommon.

With such absurdly high ideals setting the standards, when people look at their own lives at any given point they can only be disappointed by how they measure up. Your partner may well be great, but not the perfect lover or friend of your dreams. Your children may stubbornly refuse to grow up without problems. Work can be a grind. And those foreign holidays can be the source of as much stress as sun-drenched relaxation. And so, instead of accepting the facticity of the world, that such imperfections need to be dealt with, we imagine that we will have our ideal life sometime in the future.

In order to be honest and consistent we need to avoid these errors. If we think that a life without any difficulties and worries lies in the future we are mistaken. We need to recognize the fragility of good fortune and the impermanence of things. But do we have the courage and honesty to take life for what it is and make the most of it? Or do we fear that if we do so it will prove to be a disappointment?

Life's complications

At the heart of the arguments of this chapter has been a logical point about how 'why' questions and their 'because' answers generate a series of justifications, what I termed the 'why/because' series. If we see this series as extending temporally into the future, then life becomes futile, since the answer to why we should be doing what we do is always some future 'because'. If this were true, we would never be able to catch up with the purpose of life's existence and so purpose would permanently elude us, whether there is life after death or not.

The 'why/because' series, then, must terminate in a 'because' answer for which a further 'why' question is unnecessary, misguided or nonsensical. If this final purpose is itself an achievement or moment in time, however, then it may only satisfy what Kierkegaard called the aesthetic part of our human nature. Moments slip away and so if life's purpose is tied to moments, life's purpose too must slip away. So although such moments can play a part, in order to find a purpose which is truly fulfilling, we also need to find a way of living which is worthwhile in itself. In doing this, however, we should resist the temptation to see this always as an aspiration for the perfect future when, having sorted out the external factors of money and so on, we will be able to sit back and enjoy life. We need to recognize instead both that life is rarely an undiluted pleasure and that our own attitudes are themselves important to our sense of well-being.

All of this, however, is premised on a very big 'if'. This 'if' is whether or not it is possible for there to be states of affairs or lifestyles which are worth living in themselves and which are sufficiently meaningful to give life a purpose. I haven't considered that possibility here but shall do so in the chapters to come.

There is one final consideration that needs examining. I have not assumed human mortality in this chapter, since what I say about the need to end the 'why/because' series applies whether we live seventy years or for ever. The feeling may remain, however, that not enough has been said about the possibility that the existence of a transcendental reality – a god or dimension beyond this earthly one – would completely transform our perception of what the meaning of life is. So it is to this possible other world that we must now turn.

3

More things in heaven and earth

There are more things in heaven and earth, Horatio,
Than are dreamt of in your philosophy.

WILLIAM SHAKESPEARE, *HAMLET*, ACT 1, SCENE 5

Is this all there is?

Lilya was abandoned by her mother as a teenager and left in the custody of an uncaring aunt. She lived her drab life in a decrepit post-Soviet Russia, poor and without hope. Glue-sniffing became her one release, and prostitution the only available career route. Her best friend, Volodya, was twelve years old and homeless. Her already dismal existence got even worse when she was tricked into going to Sweden, where, instead of the better life promised, she found herself locked up by a man who forced her into prostitution.

It is little consolation that these events are from a fictional film, *Lilya 4-Ever*, because there are plenty of people whose stories are like Lilya's. It is a truism that life is often hard, but for a significant minority it is more wretched than most can imagine. If we are to avoid deep despair, the question of what possible redemption is available to people like Lilya seems to demand an answer.

I found *Lilya 4-Ever* intensely powerful and depressing. Despair seemed an appropriate reaction, since one is left feeling powerless to prevent such misery. There is, however, one faint shaft of light in all the gloom. Volodya dies of an overdose, but continues to appears to Lilya as an angel. I saw his presence as a kind of projection, a creation of Lilya's imagination to help her through her troubles. The angel was both a testament to the resilience of human hope and also a poignant reminder that the consolations of heaven are just illusions.

But this was not the intention of the film's director, Lukas Moodysson. 'I believe in God, and God is present in the film,' he told an interviewer. 'I do believe that someone will take care of me when I die, just like he takes care of Lilya. I honestly don't think I could have made this film without that belief. I think I would have ended up killing myself.'

Many would agree with him, believing that beyond the immanent universe – the physical world we inhabit – there must be some form of transcendental reality, a world 'outside' or 'beyond' this one. Without such a world, the senseless suffering and hopelessness of much of life within nature are unredeemed. They cannot agree with Bertrand Russell, who said, 'The universe is just there, and that is all.'

Perhaps this is simply a sign of human weakness. After all, the fact that some find the idea that there is no transcendental reality intolerable does not add up to any kind of argument or rational justification for a belief that there is some greater purpose behind the universe. Sometimes what is intolerable is true.

Nevertheless, the possibility that a transcendental realm is required to give life meaning needs to be taken seriously. Many intelligent people still believe in such a reality and their views cannot be dismissed unexamined.

Of course, some forms of religious belief dispense with the transcendental altogether. Pantheists such as the seventeenth-century Dutch philosopher Spinoza, for example, view God as being wholly immanent in creation – in other words, as existing entirely as a part of nature rather than in some sense outside of it, as its creator and/or sustainer. Spinoza talks about a single substance – 'God or nature' – rather than distinguishing between God and the nature of his creation.

Nonetheless, the vast majority of religions do postulate some kind of transcendental reality distinct from nature. So although this chapter does not cover all forms of religious belief, it does deal with its most common form.

My strategy is to consider two aspects of transcendental reality separately. The first is the possible existence of God and its implications for the meaning of life. The second is the possibility of life after death in a transcendent realm. These two issues need to be separated because one doesn't necessarily entail the other. There could be a God but no afterlife, or an afterlife but no God, at least not in the sense of a single, transcendental entity. So only after considering both separately will I turn to the possibility that there is both a God *and* an afterlife.

Although I will be casting doubt on the possibility of finding meaning in the transcendental, my hope is that those who take religion seriously will see this not as essentially a criticism, but as an honest assessment of what belief in the transcendental entails.

In God we trust?

We have already seen in the first two chapters how believing in a God does not in itself provide us with an answer to the meaning of life. But what belief in God may do is permit us to stop worrying about the meaning of life, since we can be sure that God would not have created us without some worthwhile purpose. We simply need to trust that God will take care of us. As Jesus is reported in the Gospels to have said, 'Do not be afraid of those who kill the body but cannot kill the soul. Rather, be afraid of the One who can destroy both soul and body in hell. Are not two sparrows sold for a penny? Yet not one of them will fall to the ground apart from the will of your Father. And even the very hairs of your head are all numbered. So don't be afraid; you are worth more than many sparrows' (Matthew 10:28–31).

In this view, all that is required from us is faith in God's goodness. My concern here is not to show whether faith is the right choice, but to examine more closely why such acts of faith *are* choices and what making those choices entails. I want to argue that this kind of faith involves giving up the search for, rather than discovering, the meaning of life, and should be the cause of some anxiety rather than reassurance.

If we merely trust that God has a purpose for each of us and that this purpose will prove satisfying for us, we are effectively saying, 'I don't know what the purpose of life is and I'm not going to worry about it. I'm just going to leave it to God to make it known to me in its own good time.'A person who believes that has no greater understanding of the purpose of her life than an atheist who rejects the possibility that purpose can come from God.

Consider this analogy. Two car collectors like to look for models which no one knows exist. Neither has been successful so far, but since it is possible that at least one such car is parked in a dusty garage somewhere, both have room for hope. However, the first collector decides to stop looking when he signs up the services of

Acme CarSearch Inc. Acme CarSearch expresses confidence that such cars do exist, but can provide no details as to what they are. Nor does it have any track record in successfully finding such vehicles.

It is quite clear in this example that the first collector is no nearer possessing the vehicle he pursues than the second. Indeed, his prospects might seem to be weaker, since he has employed a decidedly unreliable-sounding company to do the work for him. This example, in my view, parallels that of the atheist and the believer.

The question of who is in the better position now depends upon how trustworthy the contractor is. This is where atheists and religious believers cannot agree. For atheists, God doesn't exist, so believers have put their trust in a chimera. For believers, there is nothing more worthy of our trust than the Supreme Being. This is why even if God's purpose is 'merely' that we serve it, we have to believe that is good enough. After all, who is more likely to know what is best for us, God or we pathetic mortal creatures?

So religious believers should – and often do – agree that their faith does not reveal to them what the purpose of life is. In that sense they are no closer to understanding life's meaning than anyone else. But they can still insist that in another sense their quest for purpose is complete, since they have handed over responsibility for it to the highest being of all.

However, before atheists and believers agree to disagree, some serious implications of adopting a faith position have to be fully appreciated. That means recognizing that the believer's position is one not of reassuring comfort but of precarious risk.

The risk of faith

Having faith that God has ensured that life has a meaning or purpose for us should induce uneasiness for two reasons. The first is that such faith is by its nature non-rational. The second is that to have faith does not in any way remove responsibility for one's own ethical and existential decisions.

I prefer to say that faith is 'non-rational' rather than 'irrational' because faith is not essentially about going against the dictates of reason (although often it does) but about disregarding the usual standards of proof and evidence demanded by rationality. Faith is thus about 'opting out' of the need for rational justification rather than a deliberate attempt to act contrary to reason.

To say this is not necessarily to criticize religion, but to reiterate what many great religious thinkers and texts have said about the need to contrast faith and reason. Consider, for example, this story about faith from the Gospel of St John. The apostle Thomas refused to believe that Jesus had risen from the dead until he saw him for himself. This story has an interesting and telling detail. Thomas is presented as an example to any doubters who think that they should not believe that Christ has risen without any proof. In order to make an example of Thomas, it is not enough that he is shown to be wrong in his scepticism. He must also be humiliated in some way for ever having doubted. This humiliation duly comes when he finally meets the resurrected Jesus. The meeting itself would have been enough to provide Thomas with the evidence he needed. But from the Christian point of view, he was wrong to demand such evidence. Thus the story cannot just end with Thomas getting what he wanted. Instead, in a macabre twist, Jesus invites Thomas to place his hands in his wounds. Thomas, in being made to confront so directly the reality he has long doubted, is embarrassed and shamed for ever having doubted. Jesus then sends out a message to others who may harbour doubts: 'Blessed are those who have not seen and yet have believed' (John 20:29).

It is clear that the very point of this parable is to contrast the virtues of faith with the standards of ordinary rationality. Thomas is portrayed as misguided, but what he demands is only what is normally demanded by rational belief: the supply of good reasons – rational arguments or evidence – that what is claimed to be true is true. Until those grounds are supplied, Thomas has no rational grounds to believe Jesus has risen from the dead. Indeed, rationality would demand that he does doubt. After all, experience teaches us that people do not rise from the dead and that we should be sceptical of any claims made by others, no matter how firmly put, that they have witnessed something that goes contrary to all our experience.

So if Thomas was wrong to demand evidence, he was wrong to insist on the usual standards of rational justification for belief. This contrast is made explicit in the encounter with the risen Jesus. Once he has been supplied with the proof he craved, he has failed the test of faith. Those who have not seen and yet have believed are the ones with faith and they are the blessed. Thomas has shown himself to be weaker in faith by not believing until he has seen for himself. Once there are rational grounds for belief, faith is no longer required.

This accords with the way we usually talk about faith. We do not think it requires any faith to do or believe something for which there are good arguments and evidence. No one thinks it takes great faith to take a reliable means of transport, believe that $1+1=2$, or try and stay healthy by eating well. We do, however, think it takes great faith to trust yourself to someone you don't know, believe that Christ rose from the dead, or take an unproven remedy to try and defeat a virulent disease. All of these things require faith precisely because the evidence and good arguments that usually justify our beliefs and actions are missing. Supply these and they no longer become acts of faith.

This point is stressed by Kierkegaard in his discussion of the story of Abraham, who was about to follow God's instruction to sacrifice his own son, until, at the last minute, an angel commanded him to stop (Genesis 22). This was Abraham's famous test of faith. But it is clear that it was only a real test because it demanded that Abraham do something contrary to all he knew about morality and God's goodness.

His faith is tested on two levels. First, he must decide whether it really is God commanding him to sacrifice Isaac, or whether it is some kind of demon or madness. Second, he must decide whether to obey this voice or not. On both counts, rationality calls for him not to make the sacrifice. Surely no good God could command such a killing? And surely it cannot be right to act on such a command? Yet Abraham does act, showing again how faith operates independently of reason, and sometimes contrary to it.

This is why atheism is not a faith position. Faith is not about bridging the gap between rational belief and certainty; it is about sidestepping rationality altogether. Some may object that it requires faith to believe anything that one cannot know for sure is true, and this includes such negative statements as 'God does not exist.' But if this were a genuine case of faith, then one would require faith to believe that the Dodo no longer exists, or that Martians don't exist. This is an abuse of the term 'faith' and those who have genuine faith could rightly be offended at its implications. Faith has to mean more than this or else too much becomes a matter of faith and the shining example of Abraham and the shaming example of Thomas would cease to serve as the paradigms of faith many take them to be.

Faith, then, has to be seen in contrast to reason or else it loses its distinctive character. That is what makes it so risky. Abandoning reason means abandoning the most reliable method we have for determining what is true or fruitful in favour of trust in our own convictions or the testimony of others. But we know that these are extremely unreliable grounds for belief. In the case of religion, we know that people's personal convictions can lead them to believe in wildly different conceptions of God, gods or the supernatural.

Such differences even occur within specific denominations. The Anglican Church, for example, has been divided over the issue of gay clergy. The openly and actively gay Bishop of New Hampshire, Gene Robinson, had this to say about a row over the appointment of a homosexual as Bishop of Reading: 'I believe that those who find this troublesome are following their call from God as faithfully and as sincerely as they can. On the other hand, I am also following my call from God. I believe that there is room in our Church, in the Anglican communion, for all of us.' I would suggest he is being too sanguine and that the fact that people can interpret their 'call from God' in such divergent and contradictory ways is evidence that it is not the call of God they are hearing at all.

Faith may seem benign when it results in Sunday worship at the local church, but it can look rather more dangerous when it results in people sincerely believing that they know God's will, and that this conflicts with the views of others. This is a root of bigotry, calls to jihad or the persecution of those with different beliefs. This is why those, like Kierkegaard, who think hard about what faith means and continue to base their beliefs on it do so in 'fear and trembling'.

It wasn't me

Kierkegaard's rich retelling of the Abraham story reveals even more uncomfortable truths about what faith requires. When I was a child, the original Bible story puzzled me. This was supposed to be a test of Abraham's faith. But surely if God tells you to do something you just do it. Only a fool would disagree and be cast into the fires of hell.

But as Kierkegaard describes Abraham's agonizing deliberations, we see why there was a real and terrible choice to be made. Abraham has to ask himself several questions. Is this really God commanding me or am I being fooled by the devil? Am I just mad? Even if this is God, am I right to follow such a wicked command? Perhaps God is not good as I thought and I ought not to obey him? Or is God testing me to see how good I am? If I simply follow his command, will that show me to be a wicked person with no moral conscience? Is that his test?

Abraham has to make up his own mind. No one can do it for him. And whatever he does, he cannot evade responsibility for that choice. If he goes ahead and sacrifices his son, he cannot say, 'Don't blame me, God told me to do it,' for he decided for himself both to accept that the command was genuine and to act upon it. If he doesn't follow God's command, he can't say, 'Don't blame me, I was just following the holy law,' for he made the decision that the Ten Commandments took precedence over a direct request from the Almighty.

The story of Abraham is a parable of faith in general. What it shows is that faith is not a means of effectively handing over responsibility for the quest for life's meaning to God. If you delegate responsibility you are responsible for what your delegate does. If you choose to give up the quest for life's meaning in the belief that God will sort it out, you are responsible for the outcome.

This adds to the sense in which faith in a transcendental realm does not provide life with meaning. First, as we have seen, to place one's faith in God is to give up on the quest for meaning and simply to trust the deity. This reliance on faith is not supported by reason, but by unreliable mechanisms for finding truth: mainly personal conviction and the testimony of others. Nor does it remove any responsibility we might have for finding meaning in life or for the actions that follow from what we take that meaning to be.

This places the person of faith in a very precarious position, since their sense of security that God will look after them can lead them to give up the quest for meaning and purpose in this life. Yet that may well be the only life we have. If there is an afterlife, at least the atheist has a second chance, assuming God is not the petty vindictive being often portrayed, who punishes people simply for not believing in it. But religious believers who risk all on there being an afterlife get no second chance if they are wrong.

Life after death

Some might respond by saying that if there is no life after death nothing matters anyway. Oddly, some people use this supposed fact as an argument for the reality of the afterlife: if death is the end, life is meaningless; life cannot be meaningless, therefore there is life after death.

The flaw in this argument is that it rests on a premise – life cannot be meaningless – which is nothing but an assertion. It may well be that we cannot or will not believe that life is meaningless, but, as we have seen, our own incredulity supplies no rational grounds for belief. If life is simply meaningless, no refusal to accept that fact on our part can render it meaningful.

That leaves two serious questions that need to be asked about life after death. The first is whether or not there is such a thing; the second is whether life can be meaningful without it, or indeed whether it is more meaningful with it.

Belief in life after death can only be based on faith, since the evidence and good reasons required for a rational argument that it exists are lacking. The only evidence we have for life after death is the testimony of those who claim to have seen or communicated with the dead. This would certainly not stand up in a court of law and nor should it stand up in the court of reason. It is true, though not surprising, that a small number of these claims are hard to falsify. Among the many thousands of alleged communications with the other world there are bound to be a small number of uncanny coincidences and lucky guesses. However, if there were genuine communication between the living and the dead we would expect a great many more accurate and otherwise inexplicable communications. The fact that they are so rare suggests they are not genuine, but frauds, guesses and coincidences.

Yet these few claimed instances of communication provide the only evidence that there is life after death at all. This might not matter if there were little evidence for the contrary hypothesis. But everything we know about human beings suggests we are mortal animals who cease to exist when our bodies die. We are tied to our bodies much too intimately for it to be plausible that we are essentially immaterial souls temporarily inhabiting them. This is most evident when one considers the necessary link between thought and brain activity. All the evidence is that we require a functioning brain to have any thoughts at all. The idea, therefore, that we could go on thinking after death in some transcendental realm doesn't square with what we know about our human nature.

We could go further and say that, as well as there being no good evidence that there is life after death, the very idea is barely coherent. The question we need to ask is what kind of existence an afterlife could be. All of the possibilities present problems.

Life after death is often thought of in terms of the soul leaving the body and going on to live independently. The main problem with this view is that there is no reason to suppose such immaterial souls exist. Even if they did, it remains puzzling how this very unhuman form of life could be the vehicle for the continuation of our very human selves. It does not seem to be just an incidental feature of our existence that we are embodied, sexual creatures who use language, read, hear and interact with people. Life as a disembodied soul is a very different kind of existence from the one we have now, and it is unclear how such an afterlife could be a continuation of this life at all. Rather it would seem to be a radical break, with some very different kind of entity coming into existence after we die. Something would live after our death, but it is not clear it would be us.

If we respond to this by suggesting the afterlife is a full resurrection of the body, as some Christians maintain, then we merely have a continuation of our earthly life and the ageing, vulnerability and mortality that it involves. This provides only a temporary extension and the problem remains of how this kind of life can be meaningful.

Even if we ignore the problem of what form the afterlife could take, there are other difficulties. Our sense of self seems to be essentially rooted in our thoughts, personalities and memories. Time erodes the chains of connection that tie these to their predecessors; the person I was twenty years ago is very different from the person I am now. Because these changes are gradual and life is relatively short, we can nevertheless see our adult lives at least as forming one single narrative. But if we were to live for much longer than seventy years, wouldn't we end up becoming a series of overlapping persons rather than a single person with an identifiable life? How could I see 'myself' 200 years ago as being the same person I am now, when so much about me will have changed and so little memory of my present self remain?

All these problems really boil down to one key difficulty: when we think about the kind of beings we are, it is hard to conceive of ourselves as anything other than embodied, mortal, human animals. This is not a decisive point, but when you combine it with the lack of evidence for an afterlife and the wealth of evidence for human mortality, it really does make surviving death a remote possibility. To hope to find life's meaning in the life to come therefore seems futile.

Would that mean that life was meaningless? In some ways this whole book is a rebuttal of that claim. We will shortly be looking at various ways in which life can be seen as meaningful without any presumption of the afterlife.

It is nonetheless worth confronting directly the intuition that an afterlife is necessary for life to have meaning, for there are several reasons for being wary of the idea. One is that there is a sense in which believing in the afterlife merely allows us to postpone the question of how life can have meaning. As we saw in the previous chapter, at some point life has to become worth living for its own sake. It seems odd to suppose that this could be a mystery in this life and yet clear in the next. If one were to imagine dying and waking up in another world, how would that in any way solve the question of life's meaning? 'At last, I've cracked it!' you might yell. 'The meaning of the last life is that this one follows it!' Which invites the question, then what is the meaning of this second life?

Another reason is that it is not clear how the meaningfulness of life is affected by duration. More of something of value can be more valuable, but if something is worthless in the first place, how can increasing its quantity transform it into something worth having? An eternal life might turn out to be the most meaningless of all. What would be the point of doing anything today if you could just as easily do it tomorrow? As Albert Camus put it in The Plague, 'The order of the world is shaped by death.' The very fact that one day life will end is what propels us to act at all.

Perhaps, then, it is the desirability as much as the possibility of eternal life that we need to question. Bernard Williams suggests in his 'The Makropulos Case' that to live too long would induce 'boredom, indifference and coldness'. He takes as his starting point a play of the same name by Karel Čapek which centres on a woman who lives to the age of 342, thanks to an immortality serum. Eventually, she decides not to take the serum any more, seeing her extended life as a curse. Those who discover the truth about her agree and burn the formula for the serum. The play's insight, which Williams elaborates philosophically, is that human life is not suited to immortality.

To suppose, then, that a life after death would provide life with a meaning it would otherwise not have is mistaken. Life must be finite to have meaning, and if finite life can have meaning, then this life can have meaning.

The hard transcendental path

We are now in a position to bring together the discussion of God and the afterlife, to see how a belief or disbelief in either or both forms of transcendental reality would affect our views on the meaning of life.

If God exists and there is no afterlife, then God's existence has no relevance for the meaning of life. Whatever God's intentions or designs, it is down to us to forge a meaning for our lives and to accept or reject God's template, assuming we can know what it is.

If God exists and there is an afterlife, we can make a leap of faith and trust that God will make the meaning of life clear to us in its own good time. The problem with taking this route is that faith is a risk and there is no reason to think there is an afterlife. So in trusting God to sort out life's meaning for us we give up the quest for meaning in this life, which may be the only one we have, for a promise sustained by a trust that is not rationally grounded.

And if there is no God but there is an afterlife? Given that we cannot know this to be true, we are left in the same position as if there were no God and no afterlife. In either case, life's meaning has to be found in the living of life itself, and the promise of eventual death is necessary to make any action worthwhile at all. The only thing that becomes uncertain is the duration of life, and given what we know we would be rash to bet on its extending beyond the death of the body.

What this adds up to is the fact that there is a fundamental choice that has to be made. If we are to hold out the hope that a transcendental reality provides the key to life's meaning we cannot take half-measures. We need to believe in both a God and an afterlife, for only that sustains the hope that a meaning to life which is not spelled out by religious teachings will be revealed in due course by a deity that has our best interests at heart. To do this requires adopting a non-rational faith that is in many ways contrary to reason. It does not give a meaning to our lives but holds out the hope for a meaning that is yet to be revealed. That is why the way of faith, as Kierkegaard so perceptively saw, is not easy and reassuring, but hard and unsettling, which is why he called his great meditation on faith *Fear and Trembling*.

Do those without faith have any reasons to seek it? The rational arguments seem to stack up against faith, pointing towards the need to find meaning in the only life the evidence suggests we have. But we do not live by rational arguments alone. Like the film director Lukas Moodysson, quoted at the beginning of this chapter, many find the idea that there is nothing transcendental to redeem the lives of the wretched intolerable. That in itself can be enough to motivate the desire for faith. For the atheist, however, this is simply a sign of human weakness, our inability to confront unpleasant truths about the world and our desire to seek sanctuary in illusions.

Whichever view one takes, it should be evident that there is nothing about the supposed finiteness of human life which makes meaning impossible. So whether one holds out hope for a life after death or not, there is still value in examining this mortal life to see what might give it meaning in itself. And what we conclude about the possibility of meaning in this life may well also apply to the possible meaning of any life.

So far our discussion of the meaning of life has focused more on the possible frameworks of meaning than on the content. The main question has been where meaning could come from rather than what meaning is. We have looked to our origins, our future goals and to a transcendental realm to see if any of these could credibly be the source of life's value.

In each case, the search for meaning began somewhere other than the here and now. But the conclusion reached in each case is that at some point we need to find a form of life that is valuable in itself, with the suggestion that this mortal life is as fit a candidate as any to meet that criterion.

These considerations provide us with a framework for fleshing out what can make a meaningful life. Candidates for this role need to be worthwhile in themselves and not just means to future ends. They need to treat each human life as an autonomous being-for-itself, not merely a being-in-itself to serve some cause beyond it. They need to satisfy our aesthetic and ethical needs, as beings both tied to the present moment and existing across time. And there is no reason why such meaning should not be found in this life and not only in a supposed life to come.

For the next six chapters, my focus will be on the front-runners to provide such a meaning. We will be looking at some of the possibilities people commonly suggest when considering what life is all about. These are helping others, serving humanity, being happy, becoming successful, enjoying each day as if it were your last and freeing the mind. In each case I will argue that there is some truth in the answer, but not the whole truth.

4

Here to help

You can get everything in life you want if you will just help enough other people get what they want.

MOTIVATIONAL SPEAKER ZIG ZIGLAR, *SECRETS OF CLOSING THE SALE*

Here to help?

When I first came to London, I wanted to do something to help the homeless of the city. But my first meeting of a student group dedicated to this aim was also my last. Two aspects of the project troubled me. The first was that the group's activities were not coordinated with the work of any of the other agencies which provided more consistent and substantial help. Rather, on certain days, the group would just turn up at the Waterloo bullring to distribute food and chat with the rough-sleepers. The second was that, for all the talk of helping others, there was a lot said by volunteers about what the visits did for them. It made them feel good and realize that 'the homeless are just like the rest of us'. The fact that someone could get into a university without already knowing that disturbed me. I found myself doubting whether the group was actually helping anyone at all and, if it was, who the beneficiaries really were.

Doubts like these can arise when we think more generally about the place of altruism in the meaningful life. When asked what the purpose of life is, many will say that we are essentially here to help others. This is what allows us to break free of the pointless cycle of eating to live, living to work and working to eat. By helping others we escape the narrow and limiting concerns of our own private existence and partake in the greater good of helping those outside it. But when helping others becomes the source of meaning for our own lives, does helping others merely become a means of helping ourselves?

Many people feel that their lives are given meaning and purpose by helping others. Mother Teresa, for example, said, 'I slept and I dreamed that life is all joy, I woke and I saw that life is all service. I served and I saw that service is joy.' (Who or what she really did serve is, of course, contested.) So in a sense the question of whether helping others can be a source of meaning for life has been answered in the affirmative by the testimony of Mother Teresa and perhaps millions of others. Nonetheless, that can't be the end of the story, for two reasons. First, if helping others can provide meaning to life, those of us who are not dedicating the majority of our time to altruistic works need to know how and why. Second, we need to know whether good deeds are essential for life to be meaningful or whether they just comprise one possible road to fulfilment. And third, we would be foolish to be entirely satisfied by people's claims about their own lives. After all, people claim to be fully content doing all sorts of things: selling drugs, being porn stars, living in monasteries, running paper factories, dropping out and tuning in. We can't follow all their recommendations, so we need to consider whether their kinds of lives do actually provide meaning for us.

To find a path through these various issues, the best way to start is with the simple question invited by my experience with the students: who does altruism help and why?

Helping others to help yourself

Philosophy often makes progress by asking questions which to ordinary minds don't appear to need asking at all. One of the most infuriating of these is, 'What do you mean by . . .?' Non-philosophers tend to think they know perfectly well what words mean and can be irritated when philosophers seek to clarify the terms of a discussion by demanding clear definitions of them. Yet this kind of conceptual clarification is usually vital if the discussion is to get anywhere at all. If, for example, you are using 'freedom' to mean 'lack of constraint by government' and I am using it to mean 'ability to live one's life free from hunger and disease', then unless we are aware of this difference, any discussion we have about 'freedom' is sure to be at cross-purposes.

This is just one example of the usefulness of questioning what seems obvious. It might also seem self-evident that helping others is a good thing. Consider, for example, a case discussed by Philippa Foot of a Norwegian couple who took in a Jewish child sent from Prague to escape the Nazis. It would be very odd indeed if you found yourself asking, 'Why is that a good thing?' because you did not understand *at all* what the answer might be. But the question might be motivated by a different concern. Perhaps you are trying to think about the nature of goodness in general. You want to know what justifies classifying some things as good and some as bad. The question is important because not all cases are as clear-cut as that of the Jewish child. For example, when American and British fighters went into Iraq in 2003, toppling the regime of Saddam Hussein, some people thought this a good deed and some thought it terribly wicked. Who was right? One way to try and answer this is to get to the bottom of what makes anything good or bad at all. The best place to start might be with something which is obviously good, such as a couple saving a child, asking what makes it good and trying to generalize from there.

For these reasons we should not be surprised to find ourselves asking a question like, 'Who does altruism help and why?' As it happens, the answers to both parts of the question are extremely illuminating.

Consider first the question of who altruism helps. Primarily, this is a tautology: altruism helps the person being helped. But many people also think it benefits the person helping. Indeed, many charities and volunteer organizations make great play of this in their recruiting and promotion, emphasizing that doing good helps the altruist as well as the people they are helping. On just one page of adverts for volunteers, for example, I found the following phrases: 'Why not do something for others and gain practical skills?'; 'Live with people from around the world (and have a laugh)'; 'You can make a real difference to others. You will also make a real difference to yourself'; 'You can improve your employability while making a real difference to people's lives'.

Some people think this fact should make us cynical about good deeds. Why is helping others so often linked to helping oneself? Isn't being good precisely about *not* considering one's own welfare? Is it a coincidence that the person exhorting us to help others quoted at the start of this chapter makes his money from telling people how to make their own lives successful?

These doubts are to some extent supported by the great eighteenth-century German philosopher Immanuel Kant, who argued that one only acts morally if one does so purely out of a sense of duty to the moral law, because one sees that one is obliged to do the right thing. In contrast, someone who does the right thing because they are just inclined that way, or because it makes them feel good, is not truly acting morally, since they are not motivated by moral duty. Any good they thus do is essentially a matter of luck: it just so happens that what they do is the right thing, but they deserve no moral credit because a sense of moral duty was not what motivated them.

This line of reasoning is compelling if one thinks that the essence of morality is to follow moral precepts willingly and consciously. But if we return to the question of who altruism helps and why, we can see how this conception of morality might seem a little odd. The point about altruism is surely that it helps people and it is this that makes it good. It is not good primarily because it is the following of some moral precept.

Here the example of the Norwegian couple and the Jewish child takes a chilling and instructive turn. If we ask why their charitable deed was good, an answer like, 'Because they saved a life,' makes sense. But the answer, 'It was a good deed because they followed rules of morality,' seems to be wide of the mark. Would we think better of the couple if it turned out that before they took the child in they thought long and hard about what was morally the right thing to do, or if they were just motivated by compassion to save her? The question becomes more urgent once the end of the story is revealed. When the Germans eventually invaded Norway, the Gestapo ordered that any Jews be handed over to them. The couple then did think long and hard about what their moral duty was and concluded that they should obey the authorities. They thus handed over the child they seemed to love, who later died in Auschwitz. We would not hesitate to say they reached the wrong conclusion, but we cannot deny that they were trying dispassionately to do their duty. The mistake here seems to be that this desire overruled other moral virtues, such as compassion and love.

Those who are cynical about how helping others makes us feel good need to consider that the alternative – following moral rules dispassionately – may be too austere a conception of morality and one which is not immune to error, since there is no agreed procedure for determining what these rules are. It makes the following of moral rules for their own sake the be-all and end-all of morality when surely we need also to take into account what the effects of acting well are. At some point, we need to attend to what the probable consequences of our actions are as well as to the decision processes which lead us to do or not do them. If these consequences are important, then it may not matter whether people feel good by being good. Indeed, perhaps this is one of the consequences which ultimately makes good deeds worth doing.

We can thus approach the question of who altruism helps and why without worrying about whether there are any benefits to the person acting altruistically. But before we finally try and answer this question, we ought to consider who *should* be helped. The obvious answer is 'those who need it'. But why does anyone need help? There are two reasons we might have for helping people. One is that they are suffering from some deprivation which we think reduces their condition to one less than sufficient for a basic existence. This is the case when we help people who are sick, hungry or living in poverty. A second reason is that we want to help people who are capable of getting by to lead fuller lives. This may be because we have more than we need and can see that a little of our wealth, companionship or expertise is worth a lot more to others than it is to us. We may not notice having a dollar a day less because we are giving it to someone in need, but the money could make a huge difference to that person's quality of life.

Why is either of these a good reason for helping others? The answer must involve at least a version of the principle that, all other things being equal, the life of one human being is as valuable as that of another. If it is a bad thing for me to suffer from hunger, then it is a bad thing for anyone else to suffer from hunger. If a quality of life better than mere subsistence is good for us and our families, it is good for other such families wherever they may live. The moral impulse depends upon some kind of recognition of this equivalence between us and others. As Jeremy Bentham, the philosopher and social reformer, put it, 'Each is to count for one, and no-one for more than one.'

This is closely related to the general ethical principle of 'universalizability': if something is right (or wrong) in a certain circumstance, then it is also right (or wrong) in any relevantly similar circumstance. So if I think it is wrong for you to cheat on your partner, I should also accept that it would be wrong for me to cheat on my partner, at least in the same kind of circumstance. And if I think it would be wrong for the rest of the world to ignore the suffering in my country if we were suffering from famine, I must think it is wrong for my country to ignore the suffering in other famine-afflicted countries. In Kant's formulation, this means following the general rule, 'Act only on that maxim through which you can at the same time will that it should become a universal law.'

All of this is highly significant when we ask the question of who altruism helps and why. Primarily it helps the person in need, because it enables them either to escape dire need or to have a better quality of life. These are goods for all people, not just those who don't have them. Therefore a good quality of life is good for the person helping as well as the helped. It is good that the helper is not living in poverty as well as that the person being helped is taken out of penury.

What this should make clear is that helping others cannot be the purpose of life, because helping others is just a means to an end. We help others not primarily because the activity of helping is itself good, but because taking people out of dire need or giving them a better quality of life is good.

This can be made plain by considering what would be the case if this were not true, and it was the helping itself which were good and gave meaning to life. Holding this position creates at least three problems.

The first is that we would be in the very odd position where doing good benefits the altruist most of all. If the meaning of life is to help others, then only those doing the helping can lead meaningful lives. The people being helped are thus mere instruments to the end of giving purpose to the altruists. This would turn altruism on its head: helping others would not *just happen* to help the helper, it really would be *all about* helping oneself.

Many sentimental films positively celebrate the way in which 'altruism' redeems the altruist, with little regard to the person who is supposedly being helped. For instance, in Barry Levinson's *Rain Man*, the main narrative is the conversion of Charlie (Tom Cruise) from a selfish egotist to a compassionate, sensitive man. He learns to care for his autistic brother Raymond, played by Dustin Hoffman, and by doing so achieves moral redemption. In this film, because Raymond is beyond the emotional reach of his brother or anyone else, Charlie's learning to care *can* only help himself. So it is a very extreme example of how the cared-for comes to be a mere tool for the carer to find meaning in life.

To see altruism in this essentially self-serving way requires a very bizarre picture of the world, one that furthermore removes any dignity from those being helped, since it essentially robs their own lives of meaning. The only way life could be meaningful for all would be if we were all engaged in helping each other, in some kind of perpetual cycle of altruism. But this seems to lose sight of what the whole point of altruism is. Its purpose is not to engage in the activity of helping but to give real help. Otherwise, we end up with the old comedy staple of a person 'helping' across the road an old person who doesn't want to cross it. Help is only help if it has a desirable outcome.

There is a second difficulty we get into if we view altruism as being the purpose of living: if altruism is successful it makes itself redundant. Helping others involves meeting people's needs, but if these are indeed met there is no further requirement for altruistic acts. This presents no problem for those who think meeting these needs is our ultimate goal. But if the process of helping others is itself our primary purpose, then we are left in the odd position that were we to help others too well we would risk leaving life with no meaning at all. Altruism, if successful, would defeat its own purpose.

This paradox has a psychological counterpart in what is often called the 'culture of dependency'. This is any situation where there is a helping relationship and where the dynamic of aid leads to a situation where either party, or both, in the relationship comes to depend on its continuation. It is most evident in situations where people come to rely on voluntary or state aid, but it can also work the other way around: carers can come to need those they care for in order to give them a role or a sense of importance or value. When this happens, the carers – contrary to their explicit intentions – actually don't want those they help to become independent. This is clearly a pathological state of affairs and though its extent should not be exaggerated, it is not unusual. It does, however, vividly illustrate how seeing altruism as the source of life's meaning can distort our vision of what life should be and make us lose sight of the fact that altruism is most successful when the need to help is removed, not sustained.

A third problem arises when we remember that what altruism should be largely motivated by is a combination of the recognition of the equal value of persons and the belief that it is good to take people out of dire need or give them a decent quality of life. Without the last item in this list, we are left with a very austere vision in which everything is fine with the world as long as everyone has just enough to eat and the bare minimum to survive (although obviously this in itself would be an achievement). Presumably, what we really want is for people to be able to enjoy a decent quality of life, not merely to be able to subsist from day to day. So in acting altruistically we are motivated by a hope that as many people as possible can not only survive, but thrive.

Altruism is thus in some sense the assertion of values: the putting into action of the claim that, if it is at all possible, everyone should be able to live a full life, free from hunger and disease. If, however, the altruist starts to see helping others as *itself* the most important thing in life, then they are actually undermining the values their altruism itself asserts. How can a person claim both that everyone ought to live a full life free from suffering *and* that in his own case it is more important to help others than to live such a life? What he says is important for others is not held to be important for himself.

In applying one moral rule for himself and a different one for everyone else he is guilty of inconsistency.

This is not an argument for egocentrism, since it is not the claim that there is always a strict contradiction in putting one's own interests second. For example, it could be said that because we should count each life as equally valuable, it is perfectly consistent to sacrifice one's own welfare if one sees that by doing so one can improve the welfare of many others. This isn't a failure to see that one's own life should be free from suffering but the acceptance that since others too should be relieved of their hardships, one should sacrifice oneself as the most efficient way of bringing about the best possible overall result.

This shows why it is sometimes right and proper to sacrifice our own interests. But it doesn't show that sacrificing our own interests to help others is the most desirable thing. The ideal is that everyone, including oneself, enjoys a good quality of life. And so the ideal is one where helping others isn't necessary. That is not to deny that there are times when one's own quality of life is worth sacrificing, just that it would indeed be a sacrifice. To think otherwise – that helping others lies at the core of life's meaning – is to contradict the values that one's altruism is committed to promoting.

The germ of truth

In various ways we have seen how the belief that helping others is the very purpose of life must be mistaken. This is essentially because we have to distinguish the goal altruism strives for – improving the lot of others – from the practice of altruism. To see altruism itself as the purpose of human life is to confuse means and ends.

Nevertheless, there is something in the intuition that helping others is part of life's meaning, and so to end my discussion I want to try and draw out these truths rather than dwell on the errors of thinking altruism to be the most important value of all.

First, the upshot of the discussion is a point which may by now feel familiar. It is true that many people find helping others does give a sense of purpose to life and it is also true that the only coherent end for altruism is improving the lives of others. These two facts are not unrelated. Is it not the case that the reason why altruism feels purposeful is that we realize that people leading better lives is a good in itself? To have lifted someone out of poverty or hunger and to allow them to lead 'normal' lives, enjoying their time alone or with friends and family, is a good thing because living such a life is a good thing. Once again it seems that the ultimate goal is nothing more than the leading of life to the full. This may seem too mundane for those used to thinking about the meaning of life as some high-minded ideal or big secret, but increasingly our discussion seems to be showing that all roads lead back to meaning residing in the simple living of life itself.

The second positive is that the good feeling most of us get from altruism is indicative of something. Everyone is different, so I would not like to over-generalize, but I think this is to do with our nature as social creatures. For the vast majority of us, our lives become fuller if we are concerned with the fortunes of others as well as ourselves. As Bertrand Russell said in his *Problems of Philosophy*, there is something claustrophobic in the life of a person wrapped up in their own little world. It is hard to breathe easily when one's horizons are so restricted. Small problems become magnified in their importance when we do not see them in the context of the extreme variations of fortune found in human life as a whole. An active concern for others is in part an escape from this narrow focus, one which enables our own lives to be richer, as well as those of the people we help.

Altruism is not just an escape from the horrors of solipsism, however. Engaging ourselves with the fortunes of others is also a positive good, valuable in its own right. And for many people contact with others is absolutely essential: without it they simply wither away. A Mintel survey in 2003 came up with a striking statistic that illustrates this point: 47 per cent of people in Britain claimed to be very happy with life, but among those who lived with one or more person(s), that percentage rose to 62 per cent.

All this is not to deny that there are some who prefer a more solitary life, or to suggest that there is anything at all wrong with this. The eighteenth-century French philosopher Diderot surely went too far when he wrote, 'Only the wicked man lives alone.' For the bulk of humanity, however, the social dimension is vital to its flourishing. One reason why some think that helping others is the source of life's meaning is therefore almost certainly the truth that concern for and engagement with others are important ingredients in the meaningful life.

The third, more sobering point I'd like to make is that the value we tend to see in altruism reflects the truth that personal sacrifices may sometimes need to be made in the pursuit of a meaningful life. As we have seen, the key premises of altruism are that all human lives are of equal value and that these lives should, if possible, be lived to the full. If one genuinely believes this then it may on occasion be worth sacrificing one's own interests, or even life, to bring about a world in which more people are given the opportunity to live well. Although it is inconsistent to regard one's own life as unimportant while at the same time seeing value in the lives of others, it is not at all inconsistent to think that when the welfare of many others is at stake, one's own interests may not come first. To give up one's own life so that many others can have the chance to live life to the full is a sacrifice, but a sacrifice that can be considered worthwhile on the simple premise that life lived well, free from suffering, is a good in itself, whether that is one's own life or someone else's.

This point is worth stressing, since the repeated claim we keep coming back to – that life is itself worth living – may be wrongly interpreted as egotistical and shallow. It isn't, because it is not the claim that *my* life is itself worth living but that *human lives* (and perhaps some animal lives too) are worth living. As soon as we accept this claim, we have to accept the claims of altruism.

Helping others cannot therefore be the meaning of life itself. But it is essentially tied to the meaningful life, because it is premised on the notion that life can be a good in itself. If this is true for one it is true for all, and so we have reasons for helping others. Altruism is thus not the source of life's meaning but is something that living a meaningful life requires. We just need to remember that the purpose of helping others is to bring them benefits, not to engage in charity for charity's sake.

5

The greater good

One small step for a man, one giant leap for mankind.
NEIL ARMSTRONG, ON LANDING ON THE MOON, 20 JULY 1969

The good of the species

Neil Armstrong is not famous for being an altruist. When he became the first human being to set foot on the moon, it would be odd to say that by doing so he was helping others. Nevertheless, in his memorable phrase, the moon landing did represent a 'giant leap for mankind', a major advance in the capabilities and achievements of our species.

The United States spends around $15 billion every year on its space programme. Critics say that could fund a lot of hospitals, schools or social security. But supporters of the programme will echo Armstrong and say that expanding the boundaries of human knowledge and dominion is essential for the progress of humanity as a whole and contributes to our highest achievement. Indeed, could we not go further and say that human life can have no higher purpose, no greater meaning, than contributing to the advancements of the species?

This view has something in common with the altruistic conception of a meaningful life discussed in the previous chapter. Both views relegate one's own interests to second place. But there is a vital difference. Altruism is about helping individual human beings, sometimes one by one and sometimes on a massive scale. On the 'good of the species' view, it is not individuals that should be helped but a different kind of entity altogether: 'the species'.

It might seem that this is not a big change, because, after all, what is a species other than a collection of its individual members? But it is in fact a profound difference. It requires us to take a radically different view of what the basic 'unit of value' is. For the altruist, the basic unit of value is the individual human life. Doing good is thus about helping individuals. On the good of the species view, the basic unit of value is the species as a whole, and one can do this without helping individual humans. Consider, for example, how it makes sense to think of the moon landings as contributing to the advancement of the species, but makes little or no sense to think of their benefiting individual humans. Humanity took a great leap forward when Armstrong left the lunar module, but few, if any, individual humans on earth were made better off as a result.

Taking the species rather than individuals as the fundamental unit of value makes it possible to see life's purpose as being fundamentally distinct from one's own interests in a way in which altruism cannot. As I argued in the previous chapter, for altruism to be really about helping others, the welfare of individuals has to be the ultimate goal, which means by implication that the altruist's interests are as valuable as the interests of those she helps. This creates an equivalence of value between the helper and helped, and so the 'greater good' served is really a conglomeration of individual goods and not something distinct from them.

But if the species is the fundamental unit of value, then there is an asymmetry between the good being served and those who serve it. Serving humanity is not just a matter of serving individuals, of which oneself is an example. That means a commitment to the good of the species does not entail a commitment to one's own welfare. The good of the species could be a genuine greater good, whereas the good of our fellow human beings is the mere multiplication of a good which is no greater than that found in our own lives.

This explains how the view that we ought to serve the species differs from the view that we ought to serve our fellow human beings. Could this, then, provide life with meaning?

No such thing as humanity?

When she was the British prime minister, Margaret Thatcher famously said, 'There's no such thing as society. There are individual men and women and there are families.' Given that she was not known as a philosopher, this was a confident foray into the thorny area of ontology: the philosophical study of what it means for something to exist.

Thatcher's ontological claim lacks a clear theoretical framework. Perhaps she thought that the only things that exist are concrete particulars – in this case individual people – and that anything else made up of these individuals is a mere 'construct' that doesn't 'really' exist. But if she thought that, then why did she say families exist? After all, families are 'mere' collections of individuals. But if there are such things as families, why isn't there such a thing as society, since both are arrangements of individuals?

Setting families to one side, one can see that by her logic, one could be tempted to say there is no such thing as humankind. After all, isn't humankind too just the sum total of individual humans?

Unfortunately, ontology is more complicated than that. Too complicated, in fact, for us to go very far with it here. What we can do, however, is sketch out broadly how things like species can be thought of as ontologically distinct from their individual members without having to think of them as weird, non-physical substances. The model we can follow here is Derek Parfit's ontology of nations. In his contemporary classic, *Reasons and Persons*, Parfit distinguishes three views about the existence of entities such as nations:

1. A nation's existence just involves the existence of its citizens, living together in certain ways, on its territory.
2. A nation just *is* these citizens and this territory.
3. A nation is an entity that is distinct from its citizens and its territory.

Parfit argues that both 1 and 3 could be simultaneously true. In other words, all you need to have nations is citizens, living together in certain ways, on a territory (1). But nonetheless, such nations are distinct from these citizens and territory (3). The main reason for making this claim is that what is true of nations may not be true of its citizens or territory. A nation, for example, can be under threat of extinction from a foreign power seeking to annex it. But this power may not pose any such threat of extinction to the citizens or territory. It may be seeking an entirely peaceful annexation of the nation, for instance. So something could be true of a nation which is not true of its citizens and territory. But this is not because one requires anything other than citizens living together in some way on a territory for there to be a nation. A nation is not a separate entity 'over and above' its citizens and territory but it is nevertheless distinguishable from them. So it is too simplistic to say, as the second claim does, that a nation just *is* these citizens and this territory.

This same model can apply to species.

1. A species's existence just involves the existence of its individual members.
2. A species just *is* these individual members.
3. A species is an entity that is distinct from its individual members.

Again, although 2 is too simplistic, both 1 and 3 can be true at the same time. In order for there to be a species all you need is the individual members of it. But we have to think of the species as distinct from these individual members because what is true of the species may not be true of the individual members. For example, as a species humankind could be thriving, in that it is numerous, has control of much of the planet and is making progress. This could all be true even if the great mass of humankind were unhappy. Thus it would be true to say humankind was thriving but untrue to say individual humans were. This is because what it means for a species to thrive is just different from what it means for an individual to thrive.

This brief sketch hardly scratches the surface of the deep and numerous philosophical problems of ontology. But it does at least enable us to have a working idea of what we mean by the species and how this can be seen as importantly different from the sum total of individual humans without being something strange or mysterious. The question now is, why should we think serving this entity could provide meaning to life?

Humankind before humans

The idea that the meaning of life is to further the good of the species has sometimes been justified by appeal to evolutionary theory. But this is a very poor way of supporting the view. As we saw in Chapter 1, facts about our origins as evolved creatures do not necessarily reveal anything about how we ought to live now or what meaning our lives can have for us.

But even if one ignores the mistake of thinking that a description of evolutionary theory includes prescriptions on how to live, the claim that evolution is about the advancement of the species is just bad science. Many evolutionary theorists nowadays agree with Richard Dawkins that 'the fundamental unit of selection, and therefore of self-interest, is not the species, nor the group, nor even, strictly, the individual. It is the gene, the unit of heredity.' Most of those who disagree with Dawkins think that the individual rather than the species or gene is the fundamental unit of selection. What this means is that even if we were to allow ourselves to talk sloppily of the 'purpose of evolution', the purpose would turn out to be the survival of our genes or individuals, not the survival or advancement of the species.

To think that evolution therefore justifies the belief that our purpose is the advancement of the species is to make two mistakes: taking moral guidance from a theory (evolution) that has no moral content, and applying that theory to the species when it actually applies to genes or individuals.

The view that evolution has some kind of social application was for a while made popular by people like Herbert Spencer and Andrew Carnegie in the late nineteenth century. They thought that 'the survival of the fittest' meant that for society to be healthy it must weed out the weak and allow the strong to flourish. But this view has been discredited for over a hundred years and should not be taken seriously now, despite the attempts of some to portray contemporary evolutionary psychologists as the direct heirs of Spencer and Carnegie.

There is therefore no scientific basis for the view that our purpose in life is the advancement of the species. What else then could support it?

Another way of arguing which we can reject is the idea that we should favour the advancement of the species on the basis of some future possibility this will make real. According to this argument, we need to build upon the achievements of the past and take humankind into a better future, and this can be done in a myriad of ways, from pushing out the boundaries of knowledge or achievement to simply raising children to secure the future of our societies.

This line of reasoning falls foul of the problems we saw in Chapter 2 when examining 'why/because' series. In this case, when we ask why we should do anything, the answer is always in order to contribute to some advance in the species which represents either a small step or a giant leap towards our eventual future goal. But as we saw, such a series of justifications has to stop somewhere or ultimately it has no purpose. So the question is, what future utopian state of humanity could be so worthwhile in itself that it would justify seeing the millions of years of human evolution and advancement it took to create it as a mere means to an end?

The problems with thinking that human fulfilment will come in a future utopia are almost identical to those associated with thinking that it will come in heaven or in our own futures. In each case, the idyllic future provides an environment in which human life can flourish. But if this is a worthwhile goal, what we are saying is that allowing people to live full and flourishing lives is a good in itself. And so, once again, we find that our line of reasoning should lead us to conclude that life can have meaning now, since full and flourishing lives are a present possibility.

What heavens and utopias provide are the kinds of guarantees that real life cannot. Life can go wrong, things can turn out badly. We can strive to lead full and worthwhile lives but events can confound us. In a utopia, however, nothing can go wrong. But this doesn't mean worthwhile lives are *only possible* in utopias, it just means they are *not guaranteed* here and now. It therefore takes some bravery to confront the possibility of a full and meaningful life here and now, with the risk of it all going wrong. For if it does go wrong, there are no second chances after death. The responsibility for getting it right this entails may be hard to accept, which is perhaps why we prefer to think that meaning is just beyond us in the here and now. In another example of Sartrean bad faith, we prefer to think we have no control rather than accept that we do have a say, subject to the confines of the facticity of the world.

In any case, if we are expecting some kind of future utopia to become a reality, then we are sure to be disappointed. Not only are utopias impossible to achieve, but thinking they are possible can have disastrous results. The terror of Stalin, for example, was made possible at least in part because people were prepared to subsume the interests of millions of individuals to the perceived 'good of society' or 'social progress'. Jonathan Glover, in his excellent moral history of the twentieth century, quotes the Russian writer and human rights leader Lev Kopolev, who recalled that 'with the rest of my generation I firmly believed that the ends justified the means. Our greatest goal was the universal triumph of communism, and for the sake of that goal everything was permissible: to lie, to steal, to destroy the lives of hundreds of thousands and even millions of people . . .' Such thinking is made more possible if we place greater value on abstractions such as 'communism' or 'the species' than we do the lives of individuals.

We can see why it is wrong to place too much value on these abstractions by considering what makes anything valuable in the first place. What we usually value most are facets of reality that are made possible or can only be appreciated by feeling, intellect or consciousness. Beauty, for example, is valued, but whether it is in the eye of the beholder or not, beauty can only be appreciated by those capable of beholding it. Love too is not something felt by sticks or stones. Ideas require intelligent minds to create and examine them.

This is why the concept of animal welfare is intelligible but the concept of vegetable welfare is not. It makes sense to talk of a dog's life going well or badly for the dog. But to say that the life of a carrot has gone well or badly *for the carrot* is a nonsense. If our crop fails, the lives of our vegetables have been failures. But such an expression only makes sense if the going well or badly is related to interests of sentient creatures such as ourselves.

A species, however, is not sentient. It has no feeling, consciousness or intellect. Its individual members do, of course, but as a whole it does not. There are those who suggest that things such as species and ecosystems have a kind of collective consciousness, but this is no more than speculation and pretty wild speculation at that. The question therefore must be asked: why should we think 'the good of the species' is something valuable in itself, so valuable that furthering it can provide life with meaning? The species itself, lacking in sentience, would seem to be indifferent to its welfare. We can care about it, but why we would want to care about it more than we do about its individual members is puzzling. If we do so, we risk ending up with the kind of situation portrayed in George Orwell's satire *Animal Farm*, in which 'somehow it seemed as though the farm had grown richer without making the animals themselves any richer'.

More than this

The argument that the advancement of the species is the purpose of our existence is unconvincing if based on the promise of a future utopia, the bad science of social Darwinism or the mistake of valuing the abstraction 'the species' over its members. How, then, do we explain the allure of this view? Perhaps it is that it promises transcendence without the transcendental. By 'the transcendental', I mean a realm outside or beyond the physical world. But by 'transcendence' I mean something a little less highfalutin. Transcendence is simply escaping the confines of one's own individual, subjective existence and somehow partaking of something greater. It is simply to transcend – to rise above – our nature as finite particulars. In this way, Kierkegaard's ethical realm is itself an example of a limited attempt at transcendence from the aesthetic individual's entrapment in subjectivity and immediacy.

It seems natural to think that transcendence depends upon the transcendental. We rise above our mortality by achieving immortality in a life after death: we escape this physical world by entering the incorporeal world of heaven. However, for increasing numbers of people, there just seem to be no good reasons for thinking such a transcendental realm exists. And yet there does seem to be a kind of human urge for transcendence.

Some would say that this urge demands satisfaction. David Cooper, for example, has argued that what he calls raw or uncompensated humanism is literally unbearable. Raw humanism is the view that life 'leans on nothing'. Knowledge and value have no foundations other than those of human thought and practice. This belief, argues Cooper, cannot be sustained. Only by acknowledging that our lives and our beliefs are in some sense answerable to something other than ourselves can we bear existence. This is a demand for the kind of transcendence I have described: something – not necessarily a transcendental realm or being – greater than ourselves to which our beliefs and practices are answerable.

Cooper's arguments are long and detailed and I cannot summarize them here. All I will say is that global 'raw humanism' as described by Cooper is an extreme position, one which takes 'man to be the measure of all things' in every respect. It is certainly possible to argue that even an arch-humanist such as Sartre agrees that we are in some sense answerable to something greater than ourselves. For instance, to live in good faith our beliefs have to be answerable to the facticity of the world. But even if Cooper is right to argue that raw humanism is unbearable (and I am not convinced he is), what we need to avoid it, and hence achieve some measure of transcendence, is only the belief that we are answerable to something other than ourselves. That other could be simply an objective world, against which our claims to knowledge can be measured.

Many agree with Cooper that we in some sense do demand transcendence. I do not, however, see how it follows from the existence of this demand – if real – that its satisfaction is possible. The human desire for transcendence could be a hankering for the impossible. But even if it is not, we must not think that it requires us to postulate a transcendental reality outside of nature.

How does this relate to the idea that serving humanity can provide meaning in life? Working for the good of the species could offer an opportunity to achieve some kind of transcendence without the need to postulate the transcendental. This is because, as we have seen, the species is something different from a collection of individuals, but not because it is some kind of entity which exists over and above individuals. To put it another way, it transcends individuality but does not belong in some ghostly transcendental realm. To attach our purposes to those of the species could thus be seen as one way of transcending our nature as finite individuals. We would be giving up the claim to our individual fulfilment in the name of the fulfilment of the species's destiny.

The idea that life's meaning requires us to give up our own individuality is an interesting one which I will return to later, in Chapter 9. In this case, however, though it is possible to see the psychological attraction of the kind of transcendence promised, it is much harder to see why the species is of such value that we should give our all to it. The species may be something that transcends us, but, as we have seen, this does not necessarily make it more valuable than us. So making the object of our concern the species would seem to be misguided, for what is valuable about the species is not to be found at the level of the species itself, but at the level of its individual members. We should care for human beings, not the abstraction 'humankind'.

The joy of being an ant

Suppose we could, despite what I have argued, make some sense of the idea that the advancement of the species is a good thing in itself? After all, as my own arguments have made plain, some things have to be good in themselves. Our species, uniquely on our planet, has developed complex language, consciousness, the ability to manipulate the environment to an astonishing degree, a deep understanding of the fundamental workings of nature, and many more achievements. Isn't the striding forward of this magnificent species a good thing in itself?

It cannot be a good thing from the species's own point of view, because the species has no point of view. It is also hard to see why from a neutral 'God's-eye' view of humanity our advance would be seen as an unqualified good. An impartial observer would see the pain and destruction humanity had caused as well as its technological and intellectual advances. It is hard to understand how the advance of this species could be seen to be such a good as to provide meaning for all the lives that have been lived to achieve it.

So the problem is not that the idea that the advancement of the species is good in itself is incoherent. It is just that one struggles to find any good reason for supposing it to be true. But let us assume what has not been established: that the good of the species is a genuine good. Could that be a good sufficient to provide meaning for all the individual human lives that contribute to it?

What is interesting here is that there seems to be no fact of the matter as to whether or not working for the greater good affords life enough satisfaction. Consider how in the movie *Antz*, while the other ants around him are quite happy to get on and do their jobs, Z (Woody Allen) grumbles, 'I'm supposed to do everything for the colony. What about my needs?' Allen's ant might feel this way even if he believes that the greater good is genuinely a good. He can be entirely in favour of the advancement of the colony but think his own life is meaningless. The greater good has no need of him. Yet other ants, believing the same things about their role and the good of the colony, might find their lives quite satisfactory.

There is no strict procedure for determining what kind of contribution is enough to provide an ant-like existence with meaning. Indeed, this seems to be one area where personal impressions count for a lot. Some people, for example, are happy to do even the smallest thing for something or someone they believe in. But for every person who would be thrilled just to clean the toilet of her guru, there are others who would find being such a small cog in a machine deeply unsatisfying. After all, the species doesn't really need any of us individuals. The progress of humanity would continue more or less the same whether I live or die this afternoon, and the same is probably true of you. Very few individuals have the power to alter the course of human history.

Nor should we be comforted by the old story from chaos theory about the fluttering of the wings of a butterfly causing a tornado on the other side of the world. Some people think this shows that we should not dismiss so easily the importance of the individual. Small acts can have great consequences, so we all potentially have an important role to play. But the butterfly provides no comfort, because such chaotic effects can be good or bad and could just as easily be the result of the acts of, say, rats as of people. The whole point is that such consequences are both unintended and unforeseeable, so they hardly provide an incentive to action. All this shows is that by chance what we do may have good or catastrophic consequences, so we may contribute to humanity's decline as well as its ascent. On balance, such random effects cancel each other out, so we are left again with the conclusion that we are utterly dispensable.

If the advancement of the species is considered the ultimate purpose of life, we become like ants in a colony. We have a collective purpose, but individually only a few of us – the 'queens' – are vital. Squash any one of us and the colony carries on regardless. We gain a collective purpose at the price of removing any importance for us as individuals.

More germs of truth

As with the idea that helping others is the source of life's meaning, the idea that helping humankind is what gives us purpose does contain some germs of truth that are worth salvaging.

One is that, although in this case the good of the species is almost certainly too nebulous and dubious a goal to provide meaning to the 'worker ants' who contribute to it, there is nothing at all incoherent in the idea that we might find meaning in a greater good which we personally won't benefit from. This is, after all, the motivation that leads some people to risk their own lives. The eradication of Nazism in Europe was one cause which many considered worth giving their lives for.

This needs repeating because in my arguments there is a certain stress on the individual which could be misconstrued as egoism. The individual is important in two ways: first, the individual must be capable of recognizing what provides life with meaning or an authority which is capable of providing one. Second, the individual must make a personal choice to embrace that meaning or reject it.

These two steps – recognition and acceptance – can only be made by the individual. Therefore, in one very important respect life's meaning needs to satisfy the individual. But it does not follow that life's meaning has to serve the individual's own interests, except in the specific sense that it provides meaning for them. One can recognize and embrace a meaning or purpose to life which sees value in something other than oneself. Nor does it follow that the individual is necessarily right when she thinks she has found a meaningful way to live.

The second germ of truth is that there does seem to be a widespread, if not universal, human urge to achieve transcendence. Life seems unsatisfactory when it concerns only our individual existence. This urge must be recognized and, if it does represent a need, that need has to be addressed. But it is also an urge that can lead us astray. We cannot assume that just because we feel this desire, it can be satisfied. And even if it can, we don't want to end up embracing a way of life or body of belief just because it seems to offer the satisfaction we seek, when on closer examination it may turn out to rest on a mistake. Indeed, I would suggest that much of the appeal of 'new age' ideas is based on their promise of something transcendent, since the ideas themselves are largely nonsense.

These two legitimate possibilities – transcending the individual and serving a greater good than our own well-being – provide two wellsprings for the kind of altruism discussed in the previous chapter. Where we go wrong is to elevate the welfare of the species – which is a kind of abstraction – over the welfare of the members of that species. Human beings can feel pain, joy, love, pleasure; humankind cannot. Human beings can learn, think and develop intellectually; humankind can only do so metaphorically.

The meaning of life cannot, therefore, be to serve the advancement of the human species. Nevertheless, investigating the possibility that it might has revealed some interesting truths about what meaning does require and where the search for it might lead us.

6

As long as you're happy

*The pursuit of happiness is a most ridiculous phrase; if you pursue happiness you'll
never find it.*

C. P. SNOW

Everybody wants some

One of the most common lies in western civilization comes from
the lips of parents: 'I don't mind what my children end up doing,
just as long as they're happy.' The sentiment is usually sincere, but
accepting the choices their children actually make can prove to be
difficult. The charge of lying can be denied, however, since parents
who disapprove of something their grown-up children appear to be
happy doing can always say, 'But we don't think it's *really* making
them happy.' And of course they will be able to present evidence to
back up their claim. After all, who is undeniably and constantly
happy? Tell-tale signs of dissatisfaction and discontent can be
detected even in those whose lives are, on the whole, going well.

This example illustrates many of the contradictions and
complexities of happiness. It reflects the fact that many of us have
a tacit understanding that being happy is the most important thing

in life: 'I don't care what they do just as long as they're happy.' But it also suggests that happiness is elusive and perhaps not the be-all and end-all: the parents who say they only want their children to be happy are usually disturbed if this happiness seems to be found by working as a stripper, drug dealer or loan shark. So happiness is important but it's not everything; it's worth having but hard to possess. No wonder that the pursuit of happiness seems to be so difficult and its role in the meaning of life so unclear.

The greatest gift that we possess?

Schopenhauer wrote, 'Happiness consists in frequent repetition of pleasure.' Most other philosophers, however, have made some kind of distinction between pleasure as a temporary state of excitement or enjoyment, and happiness as a more enduring condition. So the pleasure of eating a fine meal lasts only as long as the meal does, whereas the happiness of a contented person persists in quiet moments. It makes sense to look at someone who is sleeping and say, 'There lies a happy person,' but it usually makes no sense to say, 'There lies someone experiencing pleasure.' Happiness is thus more of a 'background' condition, while pleasure is a fleeting experience which occupies the foreground of our experience. We will look more closely at pleasure in Chapter 8. Our concern here is exclusively with happiness.

There are good reasons for thinking that happiness has an important role to play in the meaning of life. Aristotle, for example, thought happiness was the ultimate end of human activity. His line of thought was similar to the one we followed in Chapter 2. Any activity has a purpose and that purpose is either something good in itself or else something which is done in order to achieve some further purpose. This series has to end with something which is good in itself, or, as he puts it in his *Ethics*, 'that which is always choosable for its own sake'.

Aristotle concluded that happiness meets this description. Happiness is always chosen 'for itself and never for any other reason'. The same is not true, he observed, for other goods, like honour. It is reasonable to ask why we would want honour, and answers may include the sense of pride it engenders, the approbation of others, or the way in which it helps make the life of the person honoured easier. But similar questions do not make sense for happiness. We do not want to be happy in order that we can do something else: happiness is valued for its own sake.

Although it is self-evident that you just don't understand what it means to be happy if you can't see why it is a good thing in itself, it is not so clear what happiness actually is. Some of the things philosophers say about it are extremely counter-intuitive. For example, Aristotle thinks happiness is 'a virtuous activity of the soul', by which he means it is to be found by living our lives in accordance with our highest nature as intelligent, reflective beings. *Homo sapiens* is for Aristotle a rational animal, not a party animal.

Even the most famous advocate of happiness as the goal of life, Epicurus, was not the great hedonist of repute. The Epicureans were serious about the pursuit of happiness but thought that the best way to achieve it was to live what to modern eyes might seem like a rather austere and ascetic life. Some typical aphorisms from Epicurus are, 'The pleasures of love never profited a man and he is lucky if they do not harm him' and 'Joyful poverty is an honourable thing.' It's happiness, but not as we know it. Or at least, not as it is presented to us in the fantasies of television, cinema and, above all, advertising. Epicurean happiness is calm contentment and freedom from disturbance, not primarily enjoyment.

There is something odd going on here. On the one hand, it can be made to seem obvious that happiness is a worthwhile goal for life, something worth having for its own sake; on the other, philosophers who sit down and think about it tend to define happiness in unfamiliar ways. I think the reason for this mix of the obvious and the puzzling is that the word 'happiness' is a kind of vague place-holder rather than a word with a specific meaning or reference. As Kant said, 'The concept of happiness is such an indeterminate concept that, although every human being wishes to attain it, he can still never say determinately and consistently with himself what he really wishes and wills.' Happiness is just whichever state provides humans with lasting satisfaction and is good in itself. It is thus by definition an intrinsic good, but also by definition unspecific. We have to do the work of discovering just what kind of states fit the description and how we achieve them.

A further complication is that it covers a wide spectrum, from the relatively shallow to the profound. A famous old advertising campaign claimed that 'Happiness is a cigar called Hamlet.' On one level, the phrase is absurd: if only life were that simple! But it works as a slogan because it contains a kernel of truth. If you sit down, relax and puff on your Hamlet, you can feel at ease with the world and experience a state of mind which is good in itself. This form of quiet satisfaction is perhaps closer to what we think of as happiness than it is to pleasure, although there may well be pleasure involved too. Of course, it doesn't last long, so it is not that kind of deep-rooted happiness we seek. But the experience is similar enough to that of genuine happiness for those minutes with your cigar to be thought of as at least providing a taste of what happiness might be.

So we might think that the place of happiness in the meaning of life is relatively clear. Happiness passes the test of being a worthwhile goal of human life. The problem is in understanding just what happiness is and how to find it. However, the philosophical problems do not end there.

Contented pigs

One complication is that we recognize different qualities as well as quantities of happiness. This is a point which the nineteenth-century philosopher John Stuart Mill made with regard to pleasure, but the same general idea can be applied to happiness. His basic insight is that 'It is better to be a human being satisfied than a pig satisfied, better to be Socrates dissatisfied than a fool satisfied.'

Since we cannot choose whether we are humans or pigs, Socrates or ourselves, the comparisons may seem irrelevant. But if we paraphrase Mill a little, we can see how his insight could apply to us: it is better to have the satisfactions of a human than the satisfactions of a pig. In other words, if the choice is between finding contentment by eating and whatever the human equivalent of lying around in mud is and finding contentment by using our more human capacities of thought, speech and intelligence, then the latter form of happiness is preferable.

Mill's choice is a simplified one, but it does reflect the fact that there are different types of happiness and some of these forms are more sophisticated, in that they are based on the exercise of human beings' 'higher' capacities and not just the 'lower' capacities we share with animals to enjoy food, sex and running around in fields. Although the choice of terms 'higher' and 'lower' might seem to prejudge the issue, I'll stick with the distinction as a convention without assuming any superiority of the higher over the lower.

The obvious objection here is to ask why we should prefer this so-called 'higher' form of happiness over its derogatorily named 'lower' counterpart. (This question is perhaps most pressing when applied to Mill's original distinction between higher and lower *pleasures*, rather than to happiness.) One answer could be that it is actually not possible to be truly happy unless we engage our higher capabilities. We can live satisfying only our lower needs, but a life lived wholly on that plane cannot usually be a truly happy one, since it addresses only one part of our nature.

I am sure there is something in this, but though perhaps not quite as much as we might think. The problem is that people who write and theorize on such matters are by their nature more cerebral in their interests than the average human being. Someone who writes books might find it inconceivable that anyone could be truly happy without some equivalent intellectual interest, but this might only show the limits of her imagination rather than any deep insight into human nature. People with raging libidos are equally baffled by the idea that a person might be content to go weeks, months or even years without sex. Football fanatics are puzzled by people who don't enjoy sport. We can see how in each case the incredulity is merely a reflection of personal passions. Shouldn't we also be suspicious of intellectuals who can't believe in happiness without intellectual stimulation?

Indeed, psychological research into happiness suggests that the keys to contentment are stable and loving relationships, good health and a certain degree of financial security and stability. These can be enjoyed by those whose most intellectual interest is *Who Wants to be a Millionaire?* just as easily as by avid readers of Proust or Wittgenstein, if not more so.

Perhaps this doesn't defeat the original hypothesis that higher forms of happiness are superior to lower ones, but merely changes our understanding of it. It could be argued that our highest capacity is not that of reason, but our ability to engage in meaningful, loving relationships with others. Interestingly, the primatologist Jane Goodall, who has spent many years living in Tanzania with not much more than chimps and baboons for company, sees this as the crucial difference between humans and the other primates. On the whole, Goodall has been much more willing than her predecessors to attribute to the primates capacities usually seen as unique to humans. For example, it was Goodall who observed the first evidence of chimps' ability to make tools when this was still considered a uniquely human capacity. Yet in her memoir, *In the Shadow of Man*, Goodall insists that in years of observation she has seen no evidence that the primates have the capacity for the kind of unselfish love possible between human beings. This suggests that the main difference between humans and primates may not be so much our rational faculties as our desire and capacity for deep and lasting love. So the philosophers' 'ratiocentric' bias – placing reason at the heart of human nature – may simply reflect their own interests and priorities, not those of the human race.

If it is a mistake to make too much of the intellectual side of our nature, it is also misguided to make too little of it. Clearly our advanced intellects are a distinguishing feature of human beings, along with our use of complex languages. But we use our intellects and languages to do more than theorize or read. Loving relationships also depend upon the ability to communicate, to think of other people and do what we understand to be right and not just what we happen to feel. One cannot distinguish too sharply between our affective and our intellectual lives. Thought and feeling are interlinked, they are not two separate domains.

Where, then, does this leave the question of what kinds of happiness are worth having? I think it cautions us against being too prescriptive. We can see that the happiness of a pig differs from the happiness of a human being. But this is not because human happiness is or should be entirely intellectual. Thought and feeling interact and so it is just not possible for any human being to be happy in exactly the way a pig is. How much intellectual activity is required for us to be happy will depend more on our own particular dispositions than on universal human nature. It is therefore hazardous to start prescribing what sorts of happiness are superior to others if we base our prescriptions on the way we see the world. Perhaps this is one area where philosophers should step aside and leave it to psychologists. They are the ones who have the evidence as to what actually makes people happy.

These reflections do, however, leave us with a philosophical problem to be solved at the individual level. Simply recognizing that happiness has different qualities as well as different intensities can help inform our choices as to how we live. Human beings have dispositions and preferences but these can be fitted into more than one form of life. A typical choice we might face, for example, is to start a family and try for the happiness which that life can provide; or remain childless and seek a different kind of fulfilment. We have to realize that making such a choice is not just about weighing total *amounts* of potential happiness but about choosing different *types* of potential contentment. And taking one path often necessarily means we can't take the other.

If we make happiness our goal, we thus have many difficult choices to make. But one question still remains: should happiness be what we strive for anyway?

Virtually happy

What we have said so far is premised on the assumption, which seems obviously true, that happiness is always worth having for its own sake, so there is no need to question whether we are right to seek it. But the conclusion of that sentence doesn't follow from its premise. For example, happiness may be good in itself, but there may also be other things which are equally good in themselves, or better. It could also be thought more important to eradicate things which are bad in themselves than it is to pursue things that are good in themselves. So, if you are about to embark on your quest for happiness and you see someone is sinking in quicksand, isn't it more important to save her first? The pursuit of happiness may be worthwhile but that does not mean it necessarily takes precedence over everything else.

Once you accept this basic premise, the question that needs to be answered is whether there are any competing goods other than happiness that merit our attention. Eliminating suffering could well be one, and, given that we live in a world where many people suffer, that may place severe limits on the energies we devote to pursuing our own happiness. At the very least, we should follow the Greek physician Galen's maxim *Primum non nocere*: first do no harm.

But even if we confine ourselves egotistically to those things that are good in themselves for us, we may find factors other than happiness coming into play. One argument that is relevant here was devised by the philosopher Robert Nozick, and comes in the form of a 'thought experiment'. Nozick asks us to imagine an experience machine, which works very much along the same lines as the eponymous supercomputer in the film *The Matrix*. Once plugged into the machine, you can live a life which from the inside feels just like normal life. Rocks feel hard, the sun bright, coffee hot, and so on. In short, there is nothing in what it is like to 'live' inside this virtual world that makes the experience different from what it is like to live in the normal world. The only difference is that all your experiences are caused not by real objects in the real world, but by computers stimulating your brain.

There is one other important difference between the experiences you have in the machine and those in the real world. Before entering the machine you can choose what kind of experiences you are going to have. So if, for example, you want to play in a rock band in front of screaming fans at Madison Square Garden, that can be arranged. But while you are in the machine you won't know that everything has been predetermined or that the experience is a mere simulation. It will feel real to you. You will be as ignorant of the fact that you are in an experience machine as you would be if you were in such a machine right now.

Imagine that such an experience machine exists. It could be possible to enter into it with the guarantee of a happy life there. The choice you have is between living outside the machine and taking a chance on happiness and living in it and being sure of happiness. And from your own point of view, both kinds of life will feel the same. Would you choose to live out the rest of your life in such a machine?

If you've answered yes, then I think you're in a minority. Most people would not only reject this option, they would be horrified by it. The problem is that they feel they wouldn't be living a 'real' life in the machine. It is not enough to have experiences of a good life, one really wants to live a good life. Visiting the pyramids in the machine may give you the same experience as visiting them in the real world would, but it matters to people that they have actually visited Egypt and not just a virtual-reality simulation of it. From the point of view of someone outside the machine, the fact that one would be ignorant of the deceit only makes it worse.

Of course, it could be argued that people's instinctive responses are wrong and that they should choose to enter the experience machine. But at the very least the knee-jerk rejection to the possibility tells us something very important in relation to happiness: it suggests that happiness is not the goal in life which trumps all other ambitions. Furthermore, the fact that most people very quickly reject the experience-machine option suggests that we have little doubt about this. If we really thought that happiness should be pursued above all else, surely we would not hesitate to enter the experience machine? Instead, we do not hesitate to reject it.

What, then, are we placing above happiness when we turn down the chance to live in the experience machine? The most plausible answer, to my mind, is that we hold dear a cluster of values which can be summed up under the heading of 'authenticity'. This is a very slippery concept, but it involves wanting to live life truthfully, seeing the world as it is and not under some deception; being the authors of our own lives; wanting our achievements to be the result of genuine effort and ability on our own parts; interacting with people who are really like us and not just simulacra. There is plenty of room for debate here about the use of words such as 'truth', 'genuine' and 'simulacra', but even if these words don't quite mean what we think they do, this broad description surely captures what many of us take to be important.

If the experience machine sounds too outlandish, the same kind of conclusion can be drawn by considering a thought experiment that is much closer to home. In Aldous Huxley's *Brave New World*, people are kept happy by regularly taking the drug soma. This future is dystopic because the happiness attained there is bought at the price of authenticity. The drug prevents people from seeing the world as it is and instead presents it to them through rose-tinted spectacles. The happiness that is achieved is not the product of personal effort and ability but the mere result of biochemistry. And the drug even prevents proper interaction between people, since everyone is not 'as they really are' but rather a drugged-up version of themselves. So we are repelled by the vision of the soma-soaked happiness, again because of its threat to our desire to live authentically and with knowledge of the truth.

We should be careful, however, not to make the mistake of now viewing this desire for authenticity as the supreme value in life which trumps all others. We may, for example, choose life in the experience machine if the alternative is endless torture in the 'real' world. And certainly these desires can seem much less important if our most basic needs for food and shelter have not been met. A starving person does not as a priority want to be the author of her destiny, she wants bread.

We must also be careful not to over-generalize. I just don't know, for example, how universal such desires for authenticity are. I think that in western society, many if not most people feel it to some extent. But it is perfectly conceivable that in some other real or possible cultures the very idea might seem alien. The desire for authenticity is not even universal in western society. I remember well talking about the soma-eaters of *Brave New World* to someone who marvelled at the wonderful lives they had. He didn't seem to have noticed that the book was a dystopic satire. But then he belonged to a significant minority of the population for whom drugs like ecstasy and cannabis are a part of everyday life. For many people these drugs are just one source of pleasure and their other desires for self-expression or what I've called authenticity are fulfilled elsewhere. But there are some for whom drugs define their modus operandi, those who think there is nothing better in life than feeling good and so if life could be a non-stop trip, they would take it. Such people would gladly hop into the experience machine.

Nevertheless, the fact that authenticity of some kind is an important value for millions of people is enough to establish that there are some things significant numbers of people value at least as much as, and in some ways more than, happiness. So we cannot assume that finding meaning in life is just a matter of determining what happiness is and how to get it.

Seek and you shall not find

So far we have found much to say in praise of happiness, but we have also cast doubt on the idea that it is the supreme good which alone gives meaning to life. Happiness has different qualities as well as quantities and we have to think about what kinds of happiness we want as well as how much. We have also seen how there may be reasons for valuing things other than happiness, even if happiness is good in itself.

Nevertheless, that still leaves happiness with an important role to play. Just as long as we achieve it without sacrificing the other things in life we value, such as autonomy and truth, and just as long as we get the kind of happiness we want, it does seem worth pursuing.

But this again is too swift. Something may be worth having but that doesn't necessarily mean we should try and pursue it. At the start of this chapter C. P. Snow is quoted as saying, 'if you pursue happiness you'll never find it'. If he is right, and happiness is a good worth having, we would be advised not to pursue it, since that would be the only sure way of making sure we did not possess it.

There is certainly some truth in what Snow says. It is commonly remarked about our own time, for example, that never before in history has the promise of happiness been so great and the reality so disappointing. Fuelled by consumerism and the power of advertising and the media, we are encouraged to think that happiness is within our grasp. Men's magazines promise happiness in the form of a six-pack stomach, great gadgets and fantastic sex, all within one month. Women's magazines promise happiness in the form of a cellulite-free body, great clothes and fantastic sex, all within one month. The images we are bombarded with are of confident, sexy people, looking smart, surrounded by equally gorgeous friends, drinking Chablis, eating exotic food – having it all.

And yet, of course, these images are aspirational. If they reflected reality they would have no appeal. Who would buy these magazines if they already had great bodies, great sex and all the consumer goods they wanted? It is obvious that the lives of real people fall short of these ideals set before us. This disparity between reality and what we aspire to cannot help us feel happier, since it only serves to emphasize what is not perfect about our lives, what we don't have as opposed to what we do. This is why the psychologist Oliver James has suggested in all seriousness that we need to severely curb the power and extent of advertising. These images are literally damaging our mental health.

The paradox is that as a society we are committed to the pursuit of happiness as never before, but we're not getting any more of it. As James details in his *Britain on the Couch*, research shows that although wealth has increased in the developed world enormously since the 1950s, we are no happier now than we were then. Worse, the incidence of mental illness, such as depression, is on the rise. It seems that the pursuit of happiness is useless, and can even fuel the kind of discontent that makes its attainment less likely.

However, if the pursuit of happiness is self-defeating that doesn't mean we have to forget about it and just hope that whatever we do will make us happy. The problem only seems to arise when we pursue happiness directly. The key is to discover what leads to happiness and do that. We will then find that happiness follows.

This returns us to Aristotle's strange-sounding idea I mentioned at the start of the chapter, that happiness is 'a virtuous activity of the soul'. What he really means by this is that we are happy when we are living lives 'virtuously', by which he means in accordance with our nature as rational beings. The key point here is that if we make this our focus and succeed in living life appropriately, happiness will follow.

I think this is broadly right. If we worry too much about being happy, we can't be happy. Better just to get on and live the kind of life we think is worthwhile and take what happiness comes from it. But we should be aware that nothing comes with guarantees. This is no foolproof recipe for happiness. There are several reasons for this. One is that more matters to us than happiness, so we can't be sure that other things won't become more important. Another is that happiness comes in many shades and tones, and we might not get the kind of complete contentment we hope for. Temperament plays a part here: some people are naturally more upbeat than others. Luck also has a role. It is hard to be happy when a loved one dies or betrays your trust. It's also hard to be happy if you're poor and living in dreadful surroundings, or homeless and living on the streets. We can never be sure these things won't happen to us, and over a lifetime some such misfortunes are bound to befall us. All we can do is have the kind of attitude and outlook that enables us to get though these hard times. Finally, we surely have to accept that uninterrupted happiness is beyond us. When George Bernard Shaw wrote, 'But a lifetime of happiness! No man could bear it; it would be hell on earth,' he was exaggerating the truth that unrelenting happiness is not a natural or even healthy condition for human beings.

For this, the wisdom of the ancient Greeks is hard to beat. In various ways many of them argued that if we cultivate the right outlook, we will be able to withstand the misfortunes that life throws at us. For example, at his trial Socrates is reported to have said, 'A good man cannot be harmed in life or in death.' Epictetus argued, 'It is not the things themselves that disturb men, but their judgements about those things.' Although these two philosophers disagreed about much, their shared insight is that how we react to events can be at least as important in determining how much they harm us as the actual events themselves.

Perhaps the greatest obstacle to happiness is the modern myth of happiness itself. If we have an unrealistic expectation of what happiness is we will never feel truly happy, even if we have as much or more than anyone could reasonably hope for. We are in danger of expecting almost as a matter of right those things in life which no one can take for granted. It sounds old-fashioned, and perhaps it is, but we have forgotten how to be thankful for what we've got and instead only know how to be resentful about what we haven't. Our desire for happiness is like a craving that we think can only be satisfied by feeding it more. Yet it is the craving that is the problem.

7

Becoming a contender

Being a contender

When Marlon Brando, as Terry Malloy, delivers his famous 'contender' speech in *On the Waterfront*, it would be far too glib to say he is relating the tragedy of a man who never became happy. Malloy's lament is not for the happy life he never had but for his lost potential. He could have had success, he could have achieved something, been 'somebody'. Yet he remained a nobody.

The desire to achieve, to fulfil our full potential, can be distinguished from the desire for happiness or pleasure. We may crave success because we think it will make us happy, but in that case success is just a means to an end. We might also crave success because we think it will bring us greater pleasures, an idea I deal with in the next chapter.

In this chapter I want to concentrate on the idea that success or achievement *itself* is what makes life meaningful, regardless of how happy it makes us or what pleasures such success affords. To establish this as a credible hypothesis, we need to consider what it really means and whether or not people should make its attainment their life's goal.

An anatomy of success

One type of success is reaching a certain level of achievement. This can be relative or absolute. For example, consider a person who wants to achieve success as a violinist. She could set herself some kind of relative goal: she wants to become good enough to earn her living full-time from playing or teaching; or she wants to play in a national orchestra; or she wants to be the first violin in a national orchestra; and so on. In each case success is defined as relative to some expectation of what the person feels she can do and not against some absolute measure of how successful a violinist can be. In contrast, someone who seeks success in absolute terms wants to get as close as possible to being the world's greatest violinist. Any more qualified or relative success is not real success at all.

There are two ways of viewing either kind of success. One focuses on the importance of having done certain things. This way of thinking echoes Sartre, who wrote, '[Man is] nothing else but the sum of his actions, nothing else but what his life is.' That's why, for Malloy to become someone, to be a true contender, he had to actually achieve something.

The alternative view focuses on becoming a certain kind of person. We achieve in order to become the people we want to be. In this way the outward signs of success are merely the visible evidence of a more important inner transformation. The first violin delights in her appointment because it is evidence that she has become the top-rate player she wants to be. But what really matters is this becoming, this developing of the self to its full potential, not the job that goes with it.

These two views are not necessarily in opposition. Indeed, Sartre's account seems to combine elements of both. According to Sartre, having done something is the only way of knowing that it was in oneself to do it. In contrast to Malloy in the film, Sartre wrote that it would not do to say, 'Circumstances have been against me, I was worthy to be something much better than I have been.' For Sartre, 'The genius of Racine is the series of his tragedies, outside of which there is nothing. Why should we attribute to Racine the capacity to write yet another tragedy when that is precisely what he did not write?' Sartre recognizes that this might seem a harsh doctrine: 'No doubt this thought may seem comfortless to one who has not made a success of life.'

This view links the meaning of doing and becoming. It is not that what matters is to do, or that what matters is to become a certain kind of person, it is to become who we become *by doing* what we do.

We need to put in place one further element in order to complete our picture of what it means to achieve success in life. So far the examples used have been of rather public forms of success, such as becoming a good violinist or writing great tragedies. But success need not be defined in such narrow terms. We can make successes of our lives in far more modest ways. The character of George Bailey in *It's a Wonderful Life* is a good, if a rather sentimentalized, example of this. He starts the film contemplating suicide, feeling rather like Malloy in *On the Waterfront*. He had dreams, he could have been a contender. Yet circumstances conspired to confound his ambitions and he has instead lived out a very ordinary life in small-town America. Fortunately a guardian angel comes to see him, and fortunately this guardian angel isn't Sartre. The angel shows him how his life has touched others and in the end George realizes that his life has been a success after all. He has succeeded in being a good person, living a decent life which is valued and appreciated by those who matter to him. This is success of a precious sort. What we must not do, then, is to presume that when we are talking about success we are talking only about artistic or professional success.

Our anatomy of success therefore distinguishes between several types of achievement. There is the distinction between relative and absolute success: setting the bar at a level to suit oneself or striving to be the best in whatever we try and do. There is the distinction between success as having done certain things and success as having become a certain kind of person, as well as a hybrid view that links both factors together. And there is an appreciation that success comes in various forms, among them professional, artistic and personal. The question we now need to consider is whether any of these forms of success can provide meaning for life.

Successful failures

The themes of success and aspiration to succeed are explored in some depth by Chekhov in his play The Seagull. Perhaps most strikingly he shows how a failure to be satisfied by any kind of relative success is a route to despair. For example, one character is a celebrated writer called Trigorin. Despite his success, his writing fails to satisfy him, for he can imagine people who knew him well standing at his graveside after he has died and saying, 'Here lies Trigorin, a clever writer, but he was not as good as Turgenieff.'

Meanwhile, one rung below Trigorin on the ladder, the idealistic Constantine eventually achieves modest success as a writer, but is dissatisfied that his work falls short of Trigorin's. 'Trigorin has worked out a process of his own,' he says, 'and descriptions are easy for him. He writes that the neck of a broken bottle lying on the bank glittered in the moonlight, and that the shadows lay black under the mill-wheel. There you have a moonlit night before your eyes, but I speak of the shimmering light, the twinkling stars, the distant sounds of a piano melting into the still and scented air, and the result is abominable.'

Yet even Constantine's modest success would be welcomed by his uncle Peter, who laments, 'When I was young, I wished to become an author; I failed.' He takes no comfort from his success as a civil servant and refuses to face his impending death with equanimity. In his view, this is the wrong sort of success.

These characters all show how the desire for success cannot be fulfilled if we continually compare our own success with that of those who have had a little bit more. Only the most successful can be satisfied by that approach. Chekhov's characters ring true. As psychologists have observed, our own sense of self-esteem is largely generated by how we compare ourselves to our peers. Yet we tend to compare ourselves to those apparently doing better than we are, discounting those who are less fortunate. That fosters discontent, since no matter how well placed we are in relation to the population as a whole, we only attend to that portion of it in comparison to whom we are losers.

Of course, the fact that these characters are tormented by the failure to meet their own ever-shifting criteria for success does not mean that striving for success cannot be the meaning of life. We have, after all, distinguished between success and happiness. Could not our purpose in life be to succeed, to aspire to do better, even though this makes us unhappy? The problem is not that such an approach makes us unhappy, it is that it is self-defeating. If success is a shifting standard, always being set a little higher than where one currently is, then by definition it can never be achieved. The most we could allow is that a few geniuses have had meaningful lives, since they have achieved unqualified success. To say there can be no meaning of life for anyone but these geniuses seems to be to confuse the meaning of exceptional life with the meaning of ordinary life. We should continue with the idea that ordinary life can have meaning unless we have very strong grounds to suppose it cannot.

One way out of this dilemma is to accept what Chekhov's characters do not: that success can be relative as well as absolute. Of course, each character seems to accept this, declaring themselves initially content to achieve only moderate success. But having reached these lesser goals they find the comparison with higher success undermines their sense of achievement. They speak as though they accept success can be relative but live as though only absolute success will do.

However, putting this straight is not simply a matter of saying we can all achieve relative success and be happy with that. This kind of thinking is what motivated the idea that in education 'all must have prizes'. Children are to be thought of as having different abilities, and success should be simply developing those abilities as best they can, even if their successes compare poorly with other people's.

But this too has its problems. The philosopher Gilbert Ryle, writing on a rather different topic, pointed out that the concept of counterfeit coins only makes sense if there are real coins to contrast them with. Likewise, the concept of success only makes sense if there is something that would count as failure. This doesn't mean that there has to be actual failure. There can be a test, for example, with a pass mark of 50 per cent which everyone happens to pass. The point is rather that there must be a genuine possibility of failure, or else success isn't success at all.

So if we define success in such a way that everyone is bound to achieve it, it becomes meaningless. We end up patronizing people by telling them that they have been successful when they know their 'success' was nothing. In *The Seagull*, the phlegmatic Doctor Eugene tries to comfort the discontented old Peter by saying, 'You wished to become State Councillor, and you are one!' Peter replies, 'I didn't try for that, it came of its own accord.' That doesn't count as a success, because it was not something he strove for and had he not become state councillor he would not have counted that as a failure.

So even if we are to count relative success as providing a meaning for life, we are still left with the problem that it condemns many of us to lead lives without meaning.

There is a further problem, one we examined in Chapter 2. If success is about achieving something in the future, where does that leave us once we have succeeded, if we do? Once we get what we want, what point is there left to life? Paradoxically, it would seem that if success is the goal of life, then once we get it we no longer have a reason to live. But how can the meaning of life be that which makes life no longer worth living? I'll say a little more about this shortly.

Is there a way out of these conundrums? In *The Seagull*, we are not left without hope. The aspiring actress Nina says near the end of the play, 'I know now, I understand at last, Constantine, that for us, whether we write or act, it is not the honour and glory of which I have dreamt that is important, it is the strength to endure.' Nina is not riding high in her acting career. Her striving has also transformed her from a carefree, joyous young woman into a darker, more troubled and battle-worn person. Happiness and professional success have eluded her. But acting has provided her with a 'calling', one which shapes her plans and dreams and gives meaning and direction to her life.

Nina's position reflects the distinction we made between success as doing and success as becoming. In one sense, she is not yet a success, in that she is not recognized as a great actress and she is still struggling to make a living acting even at a lowly level. But while Peter did not succeed in becoming a writer, and his dream was unfulfilled, she has at least *become* an actress, which is something she always dreamed of. Her success in becoming an actress does not depend on how much recognition her acting brings her. This success of becoming can never be taken away just as long as she continues to do, to act. Hence the 'struggle' she talks about. What matters is not 'honour and glory' but being what she wants to be – an actress – by doing.

Nina contrasts with the older actress Irina, who trades on past glories, inflating her rather modest achievements. Irina no longer acts, and in that sense has given up the struggle to 'become' an actress. She did once become an actress and enjoyed some fame, but she was not a truly great actress and all her triumphs are in the past. Irina is not unhappy, bitter or twisted, like Gloria Swanson's character in *Sunset Boulevard*. But she is shallow compared to some other characters and her life seems empty.

If success is about becoming through doing, it does not, then, just contrast with having once been successful, it also contrasts with once having become something. As Jonathan Rée explains in his perceptive discussion of Kierkegaard, this kind of becoming is a process which can never end. In order to become what we seek to be we need to continue that becoming or we cease to be what we once became.

Why should this kind of becoming be thought of as desirable, as even providing a meaning for life? The reason is that it fits in with much of what we saw in the last chapter as providing rivals to happiness for meaning in life. We want to live 'authentically' and we want to 'self-actualize'. This means we don't just want life to be a good ride, we want to face life honestly and become what we have the potential to become. If we want to become actors, for example, then we really do want to *become* actors, not just to have a fake experience of being an actor. Consider this choice. We could enter the experience machine with the guarantee that we'll achieve success as actors there; or we could take our chances in the real world, doing the best we can in the field of acting with no guarantees of success. Many, probably most of us, would take the second choice. It matters to us that we become what we become through our own volition and effort. This desire for self-development seems to be something we value in itself, and not just because we think it will make us happy. Like Nina, we think the struggle itself forms part of the project of finding meaning in life.

Think again about Brando's 'contender' speech and this rings true. The former boxer Malloy is a tragic figure, not so much because he failed to achieve in boxing but because he has effectively given up on becoming anything at all. He just gets by, covering his back and doing what he needs to do. But he is ultimately redeemed, not only because he succeeds in breaking the union's hold over the dockers, but because in his courage to undertake the struggle, he finds within him lost dignity and purpose. Being Hollywood, a visible success is needed to conclude the story. From a character point of view, however, the redemption is not conditional on this success, but depends solely on the resumption of Malloy's struggle to be someone, to be a contender. That allows him, before his public triumph in the final reel, to reassess himself: 'They always said I was a bum. Well, I ain't a bum, Edie.' He once became a bum, but is a bum no more. Becoming is an ongoing process and one which can be reversed.

True success

There are several types of success which by themselves cannot provide life with meaning. If we think only absolute success can make life meaningful, we must therefore accept that life is meaningless for almost everyone. Even if we allowed that relative success is what makes life meaningful, because success only counts if failure is a realistic option, we would still condemn many people to live meaningless lives. We should only go down this pessimistic route if we really have to.

On either measure of success – relative or absolute – merely having done something, to have achieved some level of success, is generally not enough to give life meaning. Achievements come and go and if our purpose is to attain them, what is left after we have done so?

As usual, it is foolish to make too hard and fast a rule. There are some achievements which can perhaps give enough lasting satisfaction to contribute to the meaningful life. Winning football's

World Cup or a Nobel Prize, for instance, might be considered such a success that if the winners achieved nothing else for the rest of their lives, they would have made their lives worthwhile. One reason why such major success might provide a more enduring sense of achievement is that it facilitates an irreversible form of becoming. To have reached the top means that a person has become one of history's greats. Once a World Cup-winner, always a World Cup-winner; once a Nobel laureate, always a Nobel laureate. So perhaps there are times when a single major achievement provides meaning for the whole of life, because it enables you to become something you will always continue to be. Not everyone will get such a lasting effect from these kinds of achievement, though, and nor do most people tend to just sit back and retire after such successes. They still feel the need to do something to keep their days purposeful.

The most plausible sense in which success can give meaning to life is the sense in which we can succeed in becoming who we want to be, and we can achieve this only by doing. This kind of success is more of a process than the achievement of an outcome. It is what Chekhov's Nina calls a 'struggle'. It has the merit of placing meaning within anyone's grasp, since there is no limit to what we might seek to become. Whether we want to become good parents, teachers, artists, firefighters or just decent people, life can have meaning if we strive to be who we want to be by doing what is necessary to become that person. The key idea here is that we are the 'authors of our own being', that we forge our own identities.

This may seem far removed from the ordinary idea of success, but it is really not so distant. It does seem legitimate, when comparing a washed-up, alcoholic Oscar®-winner and a contented family man, for example, to wonder who has made the greater success of their life. Our ordinary idea of 'success' is not so limited as not to apply to life and love as well as work and art. And we also know that the judgement each person makes on her life is ultimately about the person they are as much as what they have done. When Malloy first condemns himself for being a bum and then becomes a bum no more, his concern is with the person he is at the time, and only indirectly with the deeds he has or hasn't done. So the idea that success in life is about becoming a certain kind of person is not a distortion of the ordinary meaning of success. It is just a less shallow understanding than that which simply looks at the list of a person's visible achievements.

There is another important respect in which inner and outer success are linked. As we have seen, we only become by doing, and some of this doing can lead to tangible achievements. To do well in any field, to win recognition and awards, one usually needs to engage in the struggle to become what one seeks to be. There are always a few exceptional people who stumble into success without really trying. But most of us need to work upon ourselves in order to become what we desire to be. This struggle must itself be worthwhile or else any feeling of success will be elusive. It is a necessary condition of visible success, but public recognition is not what makes it worthwhile. Nevertheless, if it results in outward success, that can be deeply satisfying. Partly, this is because it provides external validation or recognition of what one has become. This can be extremely important for people. Many of us do not feel that our achievements are real until they have been so validated. We would be wise to resist this feeling and learn to value what we are without the need for recognition from others. But no matter how much we try and reduce our dependence on their appreciation, most of us still find such recognition satisfying if it comes, not because it is itself the goal we strive towards, but because it is external evidence that we have become what we sought to become.

Are you free?

At this point I need to make a short digression to address what may for some readers have become a nagging concern. I have often talked about such ideas as 'choosing for ourselves', 'making autonomous choices' and 'living authentically'. The unavoidability of making our own decisions and taking responsibility for our own lives is at the heart of the ongoing argument of this book. This would seem to presuppose that we have free will. But what if we don't? Wouldn't that undermine everything I have said so far?

The possibility that we don't have free will – at least as we ordinarily think of it – is not outlandish. Free will is usually thought of as the capacity to choose otherwise than we actually do. I am offered tea or coffee, for example, and my having free will is supposed to mean that I could choose either. If I take the tea I can rest assured that I could just as easily have chosen the coffee.

But the problem is that we seem to live in a universe where every physical event has a physical cause. Furthermore, there is what is known as the 'causal closure of the physical domain', meaning that everything within the physical world is caused by physical events and nothing else. Add to this the fact that all our actions involve physical movements. Even private thoughts involve physical brain events. Put these facts together and a surprising conclusion follows: all our actions must be caused entirely by events in the physical world. And because physical causation is deterministic – which means that causes necessitate their effects in some way – that leaves no room for free will.

We cannot wriggle out of this by appealing to the forms of non-deterministic causation found in quantum theory, where causes do no more than make their effects more or less probable. First, this kind of causation is only found at the subatomic level, so it has nothing to say about what happens with full-sized human beings such as ourselves. Second, it does not allow for free will, because to make a free choice is not to make a random one, or one where the causes leave room for chance in what effects they have. And third, even quantum physicists do not properly understand what is going on in the phenomena they study, so it is highly speculative for others to draw serious metaphysical conclusions from their work.

So it seems we are stuck with an unpalatable conclusion: our actions are not the consequence of the exercise of our own free will but are necessitated by all the physical events that precede them. We are no freer than the mountains, whose slow movements over time are the consequence of plate tectonics. In short, free will is an illusion.

The debate over whether we have free will or not is one of the longest and most intractable in philosophical history. Needless to say, I can't begin to resolve it here. But what I can do is point out that we must not jump straight from the metaphysical claim that all events are necessitated by prior causes to the conclusion that ordinary human free will is an illusion. Many philosophers, notably David Hume, have argued for a position known as compatibilism. Compatibilists argue that even if the metaphysical doctrine of necessity is true, we still have free will, because it is simply the ability to make our own choices without external coercion or interference. So, for example, if you offer me tea or coffee, my choice is free just as long as I haven't been hypnotized or forced at gunpoint to take one or the other. It doesn't matter if at some deep level my choice is inevitable. Free will is the unhindered operation of my decision-making processes, not the view that these processes themselves are somehow exempt from normal causal laws. As A. J. Ayer wrote, 'It is not causality that freedom is to be contrasted with, but constraint.'

Not everyone agrees that the metaphysical thesis of causal determinism can be so easily separated from our ordinary idea of free will. They therefore reject the compatibilist way out. But I think it fair to say that all philosophers agree that it is not obvious how accepting determinism as true can or should affect our everyday conception of free will. It may not leave it exactly as it was, but it may not utterly destroy it either.

For this reason, we can here afford to set aside the free-will issue. I don't rule out the possibility that metaphysical arguments about necessity could undermine the everyday notions of free will required to accept the broad line of argument followed in this book. But I do think that possibility is remote, because the kinds of freedom and choice I talk about are the kinds we confront in experience, not just in theory. When we contemplate the meaning of life, we are thinking on the plane of action, of practical decisions and choices we have to make. No matter what metaphysicians say about free will, we have to experience the world as one with choices and dilemmas and we have to resolve them as beings able to think them through and make decisions. As Kant said, although 'reason *for speculative purposes* finds the road of natural necessity much more travelled and more usable than that of freedom, yet *for practical purposes* the footpath of freedom is the only one on which it is possible to make use of our reason in our conduct'.

Improve thyself

What I have said in this chapter about making something of ourselves might take us hazardously close to the groaning self-help shelves of bookshops and the modern obsession with improving yourself in every conceivable way: by learning the seven habits of highly effective people, by releasing the child within, by creating a new you in just twenty-eight days, or by forcing chicken soup for the soul down your throat.

I think the great proliferation of such books is only possible because they tap into a genuine and near-universal human desire for self-actualization. What links these books with what I have been saying is that people do on the whole want to make something of themselves, and by doing so give their lives meaning. However, my concern is that these books take this desire and channel it in unproductive directions.

For example, they may promise to make you happy. That's all very well, but, as we saw in the last chapter, happiness isn't everything and if you make its pursuit your main concern you are unlikely to get it. They may promise you success, but they may focus only on visible success, whereas real success is about inner development. They may promise too much too easily, ignoring the fact that becoming is a kind of struggle. (Though not necessarily always an unpleasant struggle.) They may present self-improvement as a means to an end – recognition, admirers and sunny smiles – whereas it should really be an end in itself. They may promise you can have it all, whereas life inevitably requires hard choices and trade-offs. For instance, one cannot become both a great explorer and the ideal parent. This is not to criticize people who go off adventuring and leave their children in the care of others, since that may well be the best available option for all concerned. It is merely to point out what should be obvious: that making that choice means giving up a good deal of parenting and so is incompatible with the goal of being as good a parent as possible.

But perhaps the biggest danger is the way a culture of self-help fosters both feelings of inadequacy and hopes for unattainable ideals. These books promise so much and they seem to suggest that it is readily attainable. It is simply a matter of doing X, Y and Z. But life is not that easy and we cannot expect foolproof prescriptions for fulfilment and meaningful lives.

At the same time, because we see this huge menu of books, all promising that we can attain success in all manner of ways, we can feel inadequate with the genuine successes we do have. Consider, for example, the anxiety a person in a long-term relationship can feel. They may well be an excellent life partner. But perhaps they are not a sexual athlete, the world's best communicator, the possessor of a great body, a domestic god or goddess. In their local bookshop, however, they will be told by book covers that they can and perhaps should be all of these things. This can foster feelings of inadequacy and, perhaps worse still, encourage them to think that, though their partner may well be pretty good, couldn't they be that little bit better? After all, 'you're worth it'.

These problems are compounded by the illusion of control the self-help culture generates. The impression builds that there is nothing to stop you being all these wonderful things but yourself. But in trying to build our lives we constantly bump up against reality. As former British prime minister Harold Macmillan said, what often stops us doing what we set out to do is 'events, dear boy, events!' The right attitude can certainly help and there is some truth in the adage that it is not what happens to us that matters but how we react. As Epicurus put it, 'The wise man is little inconvenienced by fortune: things that matter are under the control of his own judgement and reason.' This isn't the whole truth, however, since we are surely fooling ourselves if we think we are in complete control of our lives. Failures in health, career and relationships are often not because we are terrible human beings who should have followed the advice from some self-help manual. They are usually just things that happen. As the old joke goes, if you want to make God laugh, tell him your plans.

Hence the genuine and potentially fruitful desire to develop ourselves and become the authors of our own being gets hijacked and distorted by the self-help culture, so it becomes a source of anxiety and self-doubt, the futile quest to become a complete all-round wonderful person, fully in control of our health, wealth and happiness. It is no longer good enough to strive to become what one desires; one has to become more, to achieve more. To raise a happy family, or live your life pursuing your passion, no matter what recognition you get, should be seen as a success.

Successfully being the author of your own being requires you to resist the calls to lose your flab in three weeks or get that promotion in six months, unless that's what you really want to do yourself. The frantic pursuit of unachievable ideals has nothing to do with the everyday struggle to become what we ourselves choose to become. We can learn from others so should not automatically reject any advice that might be interpreted as 'self-help'. But we need to set our own agenda, know for ourselves what success really means, and not be sucked into a rat race that only really succeeds in grinding all its competitors down.

8

Carpe diem

Life is short, should hope be more?
In the moment of our talking, envious time has ebb'd away.
Seize the present, trust tomorrow e'en as little as you may.

HORACE, *ODES*, 1.11

Living for today

Some may think that to try and deal with the subject of the meaning of life in a book like this is sheer hubris. But for others even the relatively little time and space I have devoted to the subject are wasted. Like Horace, they think that 'In the moment of our talking, envious time has ebb'd away.' This is not because they think life is meaningless and we've just got to accept it. (I'll discuss that view in Chapter 10) It is rather that they think it really isn't that complicated. The facts about life, they say, are simple. We are mortal, we are trapped in the present and we could all die any moment. All we can do is try and make the most of every moment we have. Seize the day – *carpe diem*. So while we sit around agonizing over the meaning of life, you'll find them down the pub, dangling from a bungee cord or, if they're more high-minded, weeping at the opera.

Carpe diem is a powerful sentiment, harnessed to great effect, for example, in Peter Weir's film *Dead Poets Society*. The film's hero is an inspirational schoolteacher, played by Robin Williams, who encourages his students, in the words of poet and philosopher Henry David Thoreau, 'to live deep and suck out all the marrow of life'.

One truth that lies at the core of *carpe diem* is the sense in which experiences and moments are of supreme value and should be cherished. I have personally found this insight expressed as powerfully in popular music as in high art. This is perhaps because pop is of its essence a music of the moment, which gains in immediacy what it sometimes lacks in depth or complexity. What better medium, therefore, to express the nature and importance of fleeting moments?

Two examples in particular stand out. One is Kate Bush's song 'Moments of Pleasure'. Over surging piano and strings, the chorus cries out:

> *Just being alive*
> *It can really hurt*
> *And these moments given*
> *Are a gift from time.*

Like most song lyrics, they don't read as great poetry when separated from the music. But when sung, they movingly convey the sense in which special moments, experiences of joy, are both elusive and valuable, to be appreciated and cherished precisely because the march of time ensures they cannot be kept hold of, but start to fade even at the moment of their greatest intensity.

Another example comes from Rush, whose brand of bombastic

melodic rock I would not normally associate with emotionally moving experiences. But in their song 'Time Stand Still' I again find a poignant expression of the value of the moment.

The song is a heartfelt, futile plea for the march of time to, if not halt, then at least slow down. He wants each moment to last longer and to feel every one more intensely. Instead, he can only watch as those around him grow older and he feels cheated by the way time is forever using up the moments he has, until all too soon, experience ends with death.

Both songs have the air of laments, in that they deal with a kind of tragedy: the inevitability that even the most wonderful experiences cannot be held in our grasp but rather run through our fingers like water. Life is ultimately sad because we are doomed to lose the most valuable of times. Yet in powerfully expressing emotions in the here and now they remind us just how valuable these fleeting times are.

I would go as far as to suggest that the most intense aesthetic experiences actually have their power precisely because they remind us of our mortality. Being overwhelmed in a powerful experience of the here and now makes the transitory nature of existence evident and thus brings home to us the fact that the very possibility of experience itself will come to an end. Whether or not readers will recognize this I cannot say, but it certainly describes how I have felt on occasion, especially when listening to music or watching a great play.

I mention the examples of these songs in order to draw a contrast between a shallow interpretation of 'seize the day', which just seems to advocate a kind of flippant hedonism, and a more profound, bittersweet version, which seems to draw a necessary link between the joy of the moment and the pain of its passing. This distinction alone is enough, I think, to cast severe doubt on the view that *carpe diem* is a simple doctrine whose dictates are obvious. On the contrary, as I aim to show, the whole idea of seizing the day is deeply problematic, starting with its crudest form: simple hedonism.

Party on

The pub philosopher's version of *carpe diem* is simple hedonism: 'party on'. Perched on his barstool, he (it is usually men who offer you the privilege of their wisdom in pubs) will say something like, 'At the end of the day, when all's said and done, you've just got to get on with it, haven't you? Make the most of it, have a laugh, have a drink, enjoy yourself. Grab life in both hands, have fun while you can. I'll get all the sleep I need when I'm dead!' (Actually that last line comes from a Patrick Swayze film, but it is spoken by a character who spends most of his time hanging out in bars.)

It would be facile to criticize this doctrine on the basis of the poor way it is often implemented. The problem is often that even if our pub philosopher is right, many people are clearly not very good at putting the theory into practice. Many pubs count among their clientele people who are most definitely not grabbing life with both hands and having a good time. Rather, they are grabbing beer with both hands, falling over, staggering home, throwing up and waking up feeling terrible the next day. Furthermore, in doing little else but going to the pub, they are hardly experiencing the range of pleasures the world has to offer.

This should be taken not as a bad advert for hedonic *carpe diem* but as an indication that there is a certain art to the pursuit of pleasure. If we truly believe in hedonism, we will seek out the best and most intense pleasures. Hedonists differ in their predilections. Some seek sexual pleasures, others those of good food, yet others the experiences offered by drugs. Some seek pleasure in less physically sensuous forms, such as music, travel or art. It is just too crude to assume that hedonists always seek the most immediate and physical pleasure available.

Whatever the pleasures sought, the hedonistic life has certain general features. These features are acutely observed by Kierkegaard in his description of what he calls the aesthetic life, which we first looked at in Chapter 2. The aesthetic life is not necessarily a hedonistic one, but hedonism does form a subset of the aesthetic and thus shares its basic characteristics. The paradigm of the aesthetic life is described in *Stages on Life's Way*, in a section entitled '*In Vino Veritas*'. It describes a banquet to which a variety of characters is invited at the last minute. No one is told of it in advance, everything is prepared only for that banquet, and, to emphasize the impermanence of the moment, what is left is destroyed afterwards, with the host, Constantine, symbolically throwing a glass against the wall.

The Kierkegaard commentator Alistair Hannay describes the aesthetic life as one 'ensnared in or dedicated to immediacy'. The only time that really matters or has any reality is now. Hence everything about the banquet is designed to celebrate the moment and emphasize its fleeting nature. Hedonism clearly belongs to this category of aesthetic experience, because it too is concerned with moments of pleasure that only exist in the now and which can only be experienced in the immediacy of the moment.

This does not mean that a hedonist does not think of the future or have any plans. In attempting to live for the moment, the wise hedonist will realize that all moments of time – past, present and future – are for a moment the now, and that therefore the future is not irrelevant. Thus in 'The Seducer's Diary' of Kierkegaard's *Either/Or*, we see a scheme to bed a young woman unfolding over quite a long period of time. But the goal of this scheme is a moment of pleasure and not anything else. Thus it is quite possible to desire only that which has immediacy and yet work towards attaining that thing some time in the future.

The banquet in *Stages on Life's Way* may sound like fun, but during the meal each of the guests makes a speech. It is here that the irony of the title *'In Vino Veritas'* comes in, as each speaker unwittingly reveals the limits of the aesthetic life. While in the very throes of the aesthetic, their words reveal its emptiness.

As we have already seen, the problem with the aesthetic is that although we are in one sense tied to the present, in another sense the 'now' always eludes us. One no sooner refers to the 'now' than that moment recedes into the past. To bastardize a phrase from Gilbert Ryle, we can call this 'the systematic elusiveness of "now"'. It is this feature of the present which is the source of the dissatisfaction of the guests at Constantine's banquet. They are all in their various ways 'dedicated to or ensnared in immediacy' but that means all that they live for is constantly slipping into the past. They can never keep hold of anything they value, except in memories, which also fade.

An interesting objection to this line of thought can be developed from the recent philosophy of Galen Strawson. Strawson argues that the literature on the self and personal identity has been dominated by a presupposition that a sense of 'narrative' is required for the living of a good or complete life. Strawson believes that this fails to take account of the variability of human nature. Some people, whom he calls 'diachronics', experience life as having a strong unity over time. These people are likely to find the aesthetic mode of existence unsatisfactory. But there are others, whom he calls 'episodics' – himself included – who are relatively indifferent to the past and future. For such people it can not only be natural to live mostly or even wholly in the here and now, but in extreme cases seem rather odd to think of living any other way.

The empirical part of Strawson's claim is hard to assess. That there are such episodics is hard to deny, though how many is not clear. It would seem that very few are of such a pure kind that the problems raised by Kierkegaard for a life lived wholly in the aesthetic realm do not apply at all. And even for the truly episodic, there does seem to be some desire to live beyond the moment. Strawson himself, for example, is involved in relationships and projects that extend across time and so is evidently concerned with more than just living in the present.

I would take Strawson's observation to be a useful warning of the dangers of overstating the general importance of going beyond the aesthetic mode of existence. For some people, albeit a minority, life is experienced much more in the present than it is for others. Those with a more diachronic temperament need to accept that the desire to live in the here and now can be a reflection of a deep-rooted personality type and is not necessarily indicative of a philosophical error.

But this acceptance does not dissolve the problems we have identified with the aesthetic sphere, even for episodics. Both diachronics and episodics should heed the warning of Dorothy Parker's poem 'The Flaw in Paganism', the perfect, pithy companion for Kierkegaard's 'In Vino Veritas'. It captures in four lines much of what Kierkegaard sets out to show.

Drink and dance and laugh and lie,
Love, the reeling midnight through,
For tomorrow we shall die!
(But, alas, we never do.)

Parker conjures up an image of hedonistic revellers living according to the maxim *carpe diem* because they know they will not live for ever. In the words of another variant of *carpe diem*, they live life like there's no tomorrow. And yet – 'alas' – when tomorrow comes they have not died. But why the 'alas'? Shouldn't we be delighted each day we wake up and discover we are not yet dead? For those living the aesthetic life, it is a mixed blessing. Because they live their lives only for the enjoyment of the moment, there is nothing to carry over from one day to the next. Each day one finds oneself alive one therefore has to start again, seeking new pleasures of immediacy to make life worth living. The life of pleasure thus becomes a kind of toil, because you are either enjoying yourself or you are nothing. The moment is pleasurable or it is worthless. Like Mick Jagger, such people may be able to have a good time, but they 'can't get no satisfaction'. A minority of pure episodics may well be able to sustain this kind of lifestyle, but that they are a minority is surely beyond dispute.

This is the life of the pure hedonist, the person who is dedicated solely to the pursuit of pleasure. That such a life does not ultimately satisfy is no news to most philosophers, who have distinguished between pleasures, which are temporary and fleeting, and happiness or contentment – in Aristotle *eudaimonia* – which endures. There has in general been a suspicion about pleasure which is rooted in more than a puritanical high-mindedness.

Plato, for example, thought the pursuit of pleasure foolish

because both pleasure and pain are symptoms of the body being out of equilibrium. So any swing towards one will require an equal swing in the opposite direction, cancelling it out. So, for instance, you pay the price of the pleasure of being drunk in the hangover, and the pain of being ill culminates in feelings of pleasure as you recover.

Although Plato is surely right to warn that some pleasures come at a cost, as a general account this seems wide of the mark; a skilful hedonist who enjoys drinking, say, knows how to avoid a hangover. More astute is Aristotle, who is willing to allow a role for pleasure in the good life. His major insight, however, is that we must not allow our pleasures to rule us – we must rule them. When we allow ourselves to be driven by pleasure, we end up doing things that ultimately harm us because we cannot resist the temptation of the pleasure. An all-too-typical example is to have an affair while knowing it will harm the relationship that matters most to us. (It is obviously more complicated if the full-time relationship is a disaster or an open one.) Similarly, we shirk from doing unpleasant things that we need to do because we find the pain of doing them too much. Another familiar example is failing to end a relationship that has gone terminally wrong and ultimately causing more hurt and upset for all parties involved.

Aristotle's advice sounds reasonable, but of course it can count for nothing with the pure hedonists, since for them the only thing of value is the pleasure of the moment. This only shows the poverty of their world-view, since, as Aristotle argues, it is ultimately against our interests to allow ourselves to be governed entirely by our present desires for pleasure or aversion to pain. To acknowledge this is to acknowledge that we live life in more than the aesthetic sphere, that we endure over time as well as live in the moment. This truth is what the pure hedonist resists, but because it is a truth, their failure to acknowledge it means that they cannot ever be truly satisfied.

What this all means is that if we interpret *carpe diem* as a crude call to party, a belief that the only thing we should live for is now and damn tomorrow, then it is an inadequate maxim to live by. Moments of pleasure are precious *because* they pass, because we cannot make them last any longer than they do. This may be a cause for regret, but if all that matters is pleasure then all we can do is regret, and life is ultimately no more than a sad tragedy in which we cannot possess the one thing that has real value. This is too pessimistic, not least because it is not the only way to understand what *carpe diem* means.

The pleasure principle

The phrase 'seize the day' probably owes its origins to some lines in Horace's *Odes*, which opened this chapter. If we revisit these lines, equipped with the warnings gleaned from Kierkegaard, Aristotle and Dorothy Parker about seeing them as a crude call to hedonism, we can perhaps come up with a more nuanced reading that does justice to the truths they contain.

Horace writes, 'Life is short; should hope be more?' Sartre took up this theme two millennia later when he said that we should act without hope, in 'despair'. What he meant by this is not as pessimistic as it at first seems. His point is simply that we are mortal and we can only achieve so much, and furthermore we cannot rely on others to complete our projects for us. To say we should act without hope is not, then, to say we cannot strive for a better future, but that we should not allow ourselves to be deluded that the future we seek will inevitably come to pass, by our own or others' efforts. Talk of 'no hope' and 'despair' is really no more than Sartrean hyperbole.

Sartre's discussion of hope could form a useful commentary on Horace. To say that hope should be no longer than life is not to say that we should have no plans or projects. It just means we should remember the limits of our own capabilities and, more than anything, the fact of our own mortality. This thought is significant because it is what leads into the injunction to 'seize the present'. What motivates this imperative is the fact of our mortality, not the more extreme view that we only exist in the present.

This sentiment is expanded in the next line: 'In the moment of our talking, envious time has ebb'd away.' Time is precious, it should not be wasted. But again, this is different from saying that all we have is now. What is driving Horace's thoughts is the idea of life's brevity, not the inescapability of the present. Yet the kind of pure hedonism I have rejected is based, implicitly or explicitly, on this stronger hypothesis. But it does not follow from 'life is short' that 'all that counts is the now'. The leap from one to the other is psychological, not logical.

These lines culminate in the key message: 'Seize the present; trust tomorrow e'en as little as you may.' The second part is crucial. He does not say 'do not trust tomorrow *at all*,' but '*as little as you may*.' The qualification suggests that we cannot entirely ignore tomorrow. This is wise since, as Dorothy Parker's short poem shows, those who discount tomorrow altogether are doomed to awake each day with an 'alas'. A tomorrow comes for which they have not bargained or prepared.

Horace thus seems to have a more satisfactory understanding of why we should seize the day and what it means to do so than our pub philosopher and hedonist. We need to make the most of today because life is short and this day is one of the few we have, not because today is the only day we have or because we should ignore tomorrow. We need to confine our hopes to what we can achieve in our lifetime, always mindful of the fact that the span of life is not guaranteed. The traditional saying 'Live each day as though it *were* your last' should thus be adapted to 'Live each day as if it *could be* your last, but could equally be just one more in your short life.' And we also need to remember that the probability is that tomorrow will come. The urgency to make the most of today is thus not premised on the unlikelihood of tomorrow coming, but the possibility that it might not and the certainty that at least one tomorrow won't.

This way of interpreting *carpe diem* makes much more sense. But notice that it in no way provides a meaning for life. It doesn't tell us *what* to do in life, it tells us *how* to do it. However we find meaning, we need to make sure that we go about it making the most of the time we have, not frittering away precious days. As to where we find meaning, *carpe diem* is mute.

To think that it is the pursuit of pleasure which best encompasses the spirit of *carpe diem* is thus to say more than the doctrine demands. Making the most of each day only means getting the most pleasure out of it if pleasure is the most valuable thing we can get out of life. But for anyone who holds other things dear, to think that seizing the day must mean seizing the pleasures of the day is too shallow. And as we have seen, there are good reasons for thinking that the pursuit of pleasure to the exclusion of all else is inherently unsatisfying anyway.

How, then, can one seize the day without being a pure hedonist?

There are as many answers as there are things valuable in life. Love is important, and only a foolish romantic will think love is always about pleasure. A classic movie staple is the scenario where a person in love decides they must declare it, or a couple believe they must take their chance on their love. In both cases, the cry is to seize the day, not because of pure pleasure, but because love is important and life is too short to give up on it too soon or not give it a chance.

In the film *Dead Poets Society*, which took *carpe diem* as its central theme, one of the boys in the class seizes the day by acting as Puck in a local production of *A Midsummer Night's Dream*, defying the wish of his father that he dedicate himself purely to school work. This actually leads to his suicide, in despair brought on by his father's withdrawing him from the play. The film avoids using his death as a way of seriously calling into question the wisdom of his choice, and it is not obvious that given the circumstances it was the right one. But as a simple allegory, the plotline illustrates how making the most of our life might mean expressing ourselves creatively or artistically rather than just keeping our heads down and working, and again this kind of opening up of different sides of our characters isn't simply or even primarily about experiencing pleasure. Furthermore, it doesn't mean refusing to look beyond today. To act in a play requires rehearsal and practice, and it is always possible the opening performance will never come. As Horace said, you should 'trust tomorrow e'en as little as you may,' but you cannot afford not to trust it at all.

Whatever it is that we value in life – relationships, creativity, learning, aesthetic experience, food, sex, travel – the call to seize the day is the call to appreciate these things while we can and not to put them off indefinitely. Some things require work and time, and often the best choice is not to try to do today everything you want to do before you die. The true spirit of *carpe diem* is not to panic and try to experience everything now, but to make sure every day counts.

I have argued that *carpe diem* doesn't tell us what to do in life, it tells us how to do it. It might be thought that at the very least the doctrine does tell us some things not to do. Doesn't it caution us against looking for meaning in that which extends beyond our lifespan? I don't even think this follows, just as Sartre's comments on despair do not mean that he thinks we should never work for a greater good that cannot be achieved by us alone. We can see why by considering the simple example of a great humanitarian.

The story of Dr Thomas Barnardo is one which until recently every schoolchild in Britain would have known. A great Victorian philanthropist, he opened his first home for destitute boys in London in 1870, walking the slums himself to find children who needed help. Once, his home full, he turned away an eleven-year-old boy, who was found dead two days later. After that, Barnardo ran his homes according to the principle displayed on a sign outside: 'No Destitute Child Ever Refused Admission'.

By the time Barnardo died in 1905, he had opened ninety-six homes, which cared for more than 8,500 children. He had dedicated his life to good aims that would inevitably extend beyond his own lifetime. First, the children's lives he helped would be mostly lived after his own death. And he was also engaged in the promotion of an ambition – the eradication of child destitution – which he could not have hoped to realize within his own lifetime. Nor, as Sartre observed, could he rely on others to carry on his work, although in this case his work was continued by the charity that still bears his name. Barnardo was clearly interested not only in today, but in many tomorrows to come, including those years after his own death.

Yet despite all this, Barnardo exemplifies the spirit of *carpe diem*. He was driven by the refusal to allow more days to go by without doing anything to end a great evil. His decision never to refuse admission to a destitute child was a reflection of his conviction that it was not good enough to wait until you had more capacity to help someone in need: if they needed help today, that help needed to be given today or it was no use. Barnardo seized the day with both hands, giving other people the opportunity to seize it for themselves which they would not otherwise have had.

Barnardo's altruism contrasts sharply with the kind of egocentric hedonism that is most closely associated with *carpe diem*. Yet it is, I would argue, an inspiring example of how to seize the day. It shows how helping others can contribute to a meaningful life, since Barnardo's goal was to give a decent quality of life to the children he rescued, to make their lives worth living in themselves. This is not about charity for charity's sake, which in Chapter 4 I argued could not be a source of meaning in life, but charity for the sake of what charity can achieve: better lives in the here and now.

How to seize the day

The actor Colin Farrell sports a *'carpe diem'* tattoo on his arm. He told the *Toronto Star*, 'It means "seize the day", live in the moment and enjoy life. Try not to worry about tomorrow, try to let yesterday go away.' If that were really what *carpe diem* meant, then I would argue that Farrell has made a mistake to try and live by it. Living only for the moment and forgetting about tomorrow or yesterday is not a recipe for satisfaction. The problem is that pleasures come and go, and the tomorrow we imagine will never come almost always does.

Pure hedonism leaves us empty, constantly craving more pleasure and destined never to have our fill. The warnings are there, from Plato and Aristotle, through Kierkegaard to Dorothy Parker.

It's a message that we need to counter the cult of pleasure which now dominates advertisements and lifestyle magazines. They seem to offer the promise that, if we can fill our lives with enough restaurant meals, mini-breaks, holidays and gourmet dinner parties we will get enough pleasure to have full and satisfied lives. They also promote a kind of hedonistic angst, the fear that there are great pleasures others are enjoying which we are not. To have to answer negatively the question in the title of William Sutcliffe's satire on backpacking culture, *Are You Experienced?*, is to admit we haven't lived.

As Aristotle recognized, pleasure does have a role to play in the good life, more than perhaps most philosophers have allowed. But it is only one part. Making the most of today is not just about existing in the moment and it is not just about pleasure. We seize the day when we do not put off doing today that which can be done today, not when we give up the chance of doing in the future what can only be done then.

The idea that we should seize the day does not tell us what matters in life. We need first to identify that, or else what we seize may be empty or worthless. The wisdom of *carpe diem* is that time is short, this is the only life we have and we should not squander it. This wisdom is turned to folly if we assume this means that only pleasure counts, and thus spend our days forever grasping at moments in time which start to recede into the past even as we reach for them.

9

Lose your self

Free your mind and your ass will follow
The kingdom of heaven is within.
Open up your funky mind and you can fly . . .

FUNKADELIC, 'FREE YOUR MIND AND YOUR ASS WILL FOLLOW'

If we're looking for wisdom, the lyrics of George Clinton's outrageous funk bands may not be the obvious place to start. But what Funkadelic's lyrics exemplify is not some deep truth about the universe, but the popular appeal of the vague and varying idea that the way to enlightenment requires some kind of freeing of your mind. The idea may be traceable back to eastern philosophies such as Buddhism, but its grip on the western imagination has probably more to do with the 1960s and psychedelia. The meaning of life is not to be found by earnestly thinking it through, but by chilling out, opening your mind and letting go of your ego. Attune yourself to the rhythms of the universe and, assuming they are funky rhythms, 'your ass will follow'.

As I have suggested, one problem with examining this possibility is that it is not a single idea at all, but a jumble of ideas from Buddhism, mysticism, 1960s counter-culture, new-age mumbo-jumbo and self-help. A recurring theme, however, is that the key is loss of ego, the loosening of the grip we have on our own sense of self in favour of some kind of surrender to wider reality. The thought is that rather than see the meaning of life as being about what purpose *I* can achieve, whether *I* can be happy or content, or how good a life *I* lead, we should see it as being about learning to care less about this 'I' altogether. So we don't so much *solve* the problem of 'Why am I here?' as *dissolve* it by learning to see that such egocentric questions should not be asked. By freeing our minds, we see that 'I' becomes unimportant.

My concern here is not to deal with every major variant of this idea but to consider some of the most general issues the broad approach raises. This method does have limitations, which I will discuss in a section on narrowing your mind. My strategy is simply to ask how such a view could be the key to the meaning of life. Two answers suggest themselves. The first is that it reflects a basic truth, namely that the self does not really exist. So in learning to detach from our sense of self we become more in tune with the true nature of reality. The other possibility is that the self is real, but that, paradoxical though it may sound, the way for the self to find meaning is for it to care less about itself. By considering these two very general possibilities, we can go a long way towards measuring the potential of this diverse set of views to provide meaning to life.

No ego

When Descartes famously sat down to see what truths were beyond all doubt, he ended up with just the one: that he was an existing, thinking thing. In his *Discourse on Method*, he wrote, 'I observed that this truth, *I think, therefore I am*, was so certain and of such evidence that no ground of doubt, however extravagant, could be alleged by the sceptics capable of shaking it.' If Descartes is right, then not only is the existence of the self certain, it is the most certain thing of all, because all else can at least be doubted. One cannot, however, doubt the existence of the self, because in the very act of doubting, the self declares itself. 'I doubt I exist' can only be thought if there is an 'I' which is doing the doubting.

If Descartes is right, then the idea that we should detach ourselves from our egos because the self is a kind of illusion is plainly false. The self is not illusory but the most certain feature of reality. Is it possible, however, that Descartes is wrong? Many have thought so. The main problem is that Descartes is certain of too much. When he thinks, all he is really entitled to be certain of is that there is thinking going on. He is not entitled to conclude that this thinking is indicative of the presence of a real self or soul.

The criticism was made incisively by the great Scottish philosopher David Hume, who reported his own failure to replicate Descartes's sense of certainty when he tried to capture himself thinking.

When I enter most intimately into what I call myself, I always stumble on some particular perception or other, of heat or cold, light or shade, love or hatred, pain or pleasure. I can never catch myself at any time without a perception, and never can observe anything but the perception. When my perceptions are removed for any time, as by sound sleep, so long am I insensible of myself, and may truly be said not to exist. (*A Treatise of Human Nature*, Book One)

Hume's experiment can be carried out by anyone at any time. Try to introspect and become aware of your self. Hume believed you will fail. You will be aware of particular thoughts and feelings, but not of any self which is having them. Hence Hume's view has come to be known as the 'bundle' theory of the self. The self is not a single entity which has thoughts and feelings, it is rather the collection of interconnected thoughts and feelings themselves.

Hume is certainly no mystic and he did not advocate any kind of dissolution of the ego as a means to enlightenment. Nonetheless, his view does bear a striking resemblance to the Buddhist *anatta* or 'no self' view. Buddhism talks of the individual being comprising five *khandhas*, variously translated as 'aggregates', 'factors', 'groups' or literally 'heaps'. These are *rupa* (the physical form of the body), *vedana* (feeling), *sañña* (perception), *sankhara* ('mental formation', including thought processes and acts of volition) and *viññana* (consciousness). The way in which this view parallels Hume is that the self is not any one of these five *khandhas*, nor is it some such other 'thing'. Rather it is just the five *khandhas* working together.

An analogy which has been used to explain this doctrine is between the self and a cart. Sister Vajira, a contemporary of the Buddha and an *arahant* – someone who is deemed to have achieved the highest stage of enlightenment – wrote:

> *When all constituent parts are there,*
> *The designation 'cart' is used;*
> *Just so, where the five groups [khandhas] exist,*
> *Of 'living being' do we speak.*

A cart is simply the parts of a cart suitably arranged. It is not some object 'over and above' the parts of the cart. In the same way, what we call the self – the individual human person – is just the five *khandhas* suitably arranged.

Does this mean that the self is a kind of illusion? That would seem to be too strong a conclusion to draw. In the analogy, for example, it would be silly to say that the cart doesn't exist. The fact that it is no more than the sum of its parts doesn't mean this sum is an illusion. Indeed, if the cart is the sum of its parts, then just as long as those parts exist the cart *must* exist. The only 'illusion' would be if we held the rather odd view that a cart is something different from a suitably arranged collection of cart parts. Likewise, the only sense in which the self is an illusion is if we think of the self as a separate, distinct entity which can exist independently of the particular body, thoughts and feelings which it comprises. This seems to be the only sensible conclusion that can be drawn if one accepts the Buddhist teachings or the arguments of David Hume.

This is significant, because if this is the only reasonable sense in which we can say that the self is an illusion, is it enough to justify the belief that in order to live in harmony with the truth we ought to seek to somehow lose our attachment to the self? In other words, would accepting a Humean 'bundle' view or a Buddhist *anatta* view make the dissolution of the ego the most rational course of action open to us?

There is one sense in which a weakening of our attachment to self would seem to be a rational response to accepting either view. If the self is only such an aggregate then there seems little hope of surviving our bodily death, since that would destroy part of the fabric that keeps the self together. We should, then, remember that our existence is contingent on the collection which is our body, thoughts and sensations.

This might seem to go against the Buddhist idea of rebirth. Buddhist belief in rebirth – like the significantly different Hindu idea of the transmigration of souls – is extremely difficult to reconcile with what we know about human mortality and the dependence of consciousness on brains. It seems to me that the only way it can be reconciled with the *anatta* doctrine is by accepting a number of beliefs that we have no independent reasons to accept, such as the idea that the series of mental processes – known as *cittas* – passes from one life to another on death. There seem to be no grounds at all for believing this other than the acceptance of Buddhist scriptures. But even if it is accepted, it does not seem to be the continuation of an individual self as usually understood. It seems rather to be like passing on a baton of consciousness from one self to another.

So whether we go with Buddhism or with Hume's more worldly 'bundle' theory, there seems little reason to look forward to any kind of genuine afterlife for the selves we are in this life. But in no other respect does it seem rational to lessen the attachment we have to ourselves if we accept something like the 'no self' or 'bundle' view. Both views simply try to explain what accounts for our sense of self and hold that the self is not a distinct, independent entity. But it does not follow from that that we should will the dismantling of this aggregated self. We know a car is just the collection of its parts, but we don't think that therefore the most real form of existence for the car is when it is dismantled into these parts. If anything it should make us think that it is only by keeping the parts suitably arranged that we can be said to have a car at all. Similarly, if the self is just a product of body and brain working properly to produce thought and sensation, there is no reason to think we can live more authentically if we seek to dissolve this self in some way. If we think we should strive for a dissolution of the ego, we need a better reason than the belief that there is no permanent self.

Selfishly losing one's self

There is another possibility. We might think that we should lessen our attachment to the self, not because that is the way of reflecting the true nature of reality, but because that is what is required for the self to flourish. You might think of this as a kind of reverse psychology for the soul, something like the idea that if you want to keep the attention of the one you love, you ought to neglect them rather than be nice to them all the time. Similarly, if you want your self to flourish you must learn to care about it less. This idea has the whiff of paradox about it, which is often the hallmark of profound-sounding but vacuous ideas.

There are some ways in which lessening our concern for ourselves can be of benefit. But even when it is a good thing, it is hard to see it as providing anything like a meaning for life. For example, I think it is true that people find it hard to be happy and at ease with the world if they are too wrapped up with themselves and, in particular, their problems. The life of such a person is what Bertrand Russell called 'feverish and confined'. Such people do need to learn to care a little less about themselves and take a wider perspective on the world. Doing so can free them from the mental trap of unproductive egocentrism. But this at best removes an obstacle to leading a meaningful life, it doesn't in itself provide that meaning.

Another case is of the person who practises one of the many forms of meditation designed to lessen one's sense of self. As we have seen, if this is supposed to be desirable because the self is a kind of illusion, then it rests on a mistake. An alternative reason could be that the meditative technique helps a person to feel better: more calm or accepting, for example. But again, although this provides a benefit, it doesn't provide a meaning for life. We would need to ask why we think feeling calmer and more accepting of our place in the world helps to give our lives more meaning. After all, couldn't it be argued that such feelings promote resignation to whatever happens in life rather than full engagement with it? Could this be what Nietzsche calls a life-denying philosophy, one that makes us turn our backs on the struggle that living life to the full requires and instead pacifies us, leaving us with something less? These questions need to be answered. It is not enough to conclude, from the fact that people report benefits from forms of meditation which encourage a lessening of their sense of self, that therefore such forms of meditation can give meaning to life.

A third possible explanation as to why we should try and lose our sense of self is that by doing so we achieve oneness with the universe. We lose our own individuality and instead feel ourselves to be part of the great whole that is existence.

Once again I am going to be brisk with an idea that many will feel deserves more serious attention. But this whole notion is just incoherent. If one genuinely lost one's sense of self, one would not be able to report any feeling of oneness with the universe. Rather, at the end of the meditation, one would report coming back to awareness after having lost any sense of consciousness, a bit like the way one feels after waking up. Any euphoric feelings during such a form of meditation have to be had by *oneself* or else there can be no feelings at all.

A further problem with this idea is that it suggests the meaning of a person's life is not to have a life at all. You reach your highest potential by losing your sense of self altogether – in effect, by ceasing to exist. We end up with another impressive-sounding paradox: the meaning of your life is for you to lose all sense of that life. Well, that can be arranged – it's called death.

The reason I am being a little brutal here is that I think there is a terrible dishonesty among some of those who claim that what they are trying to achieve is a lessening of attachment to ego. The clear truth is that people who find this path satisfying are living contented lives. In other words, they like their 'spiritual practices' because these make them feel more content, at peace, or whatever, than alternatives they have tried. So despite all the fine words about losing their egos, they are in fact simply engaging in another form of self-gratification. This isn't materialistic or harmful to others, so we tend to look upon it quite kindly. But it is not in any sense a way of life which shows disregard for self-interest.

Indeed, it is striking how any mention of a word like 'soul' or 'spirit' can blind us to the presence of egocentrism. Madonna, for example, once said, 'Our job is to navigate through this world while understanding that the only thing that matters is the state of our soul.' That may make her sound very 'spiritual' but she is expressing an entirely self-centred attitude. The 'only thing that matters' is how we are, ourselves, inside.

The person who endures hardship to help others shows considerably more disregard for their own welfare than a person who lives smiling and at peace in a monastery or commune. Whichever way you look at it, this is about satisfying the self, not lessening concern for it. It may be a worthwhile form of life, but it must be seen for what it is.

There are those who say that meditation can give us a form of knowledge which cannot be expressed in words. In which case, as Wittgenstein said, 'What we cannot talk about we must pass over in silence.' I confess myself to be a sceptic, and this scepticism is bolstered by the fact that since words cannot express what this enlightenment is supposed to be like or of, I have no grounds on which to judge whether I should give it a go myself. After all, similar promises are made of many and varying forms of spirituality. They usually also stress that it takes many years to achieve this illumination. But then what reasons could I be given to make me choose one way over another and dedicate years of my life to the pursuit of something I know not what it is? It can only be that I am impressed by the effect it seems to have on others and have good reason to want to be like them and to think that I can be like them. Personally, however, I tend to find that the kind of detachment many such people have seems smug, self-righteous and alienating.

I would nonetheless acknowledge the possible truths that lie behind these spiritual practices. I can see that meditation might form part of a meaningful life, in the same way that I see how happiness, pleasure, the pursuit of excellence and love can form part of a meaningful life. All these things can help make this life we have worth living in itself. But they can all only be judged according to how they do or do not contribute to this goal.

So, for example, let us imagine that someone does feel a profound peace in meditation, or a sense of oneness with the universe. These feelings may be such that the person thinks that just being able to have them makes life worthwhile. She is thus able to lead what for her is a meaningful life because she has found a mode of living which is worthwhile in itself. Only in this way can the benefits of meditation be said to contribute to a meaningful life.

But it has to be remembered that what is reported are subjective feelings, not facts. If someone says she *feels* she is at one with the universe, that doesn't mean that she *is*, any more than someone saying she has heard the voice of God means she has. Such feelings are no guide to the truth. And, as we have seen, one thing most of us want from life is to live it truthfully. We don't want to be fooled as to the nature of reality. I think that people feel their meditation makes their life meaningful not just because it is a great experience, but because they think it offers them some kind of awareness of truth. Despite the apparent contradictions I identified earlier, they think their so-called loss of sense of self reflects some truth about the self.

On this there is little to be said. These claims are made not on the basis of reasons that can be explained but on that of personal conviction, grounded in subjective experience. This places the person in the same position as anyone who believes on the basis of faith. And as I argued in Chapter 3, such faith is a risk since it rests on a form of justification that is generally unreliable. In this case, where the type of knowledge claimed is specified as that which cannot be expressed in words, there is nothing one can say directly about the object of this faith. All one can say is that people who claim this kind of knowledge should recognize that no matter how strong their personal convictions, they cannot be considered in general to provide good reasons for others to follow them, or even good reasons for themselves to believe.

Narrow your mind

I am certain that many will find my dismissal of the view that we ought to lessen our attachment to our egos or selves far too cursory.

It might correctly be pointed out that, coming from the western philosophical tradition, I simply don't know a great deal about many of the eastern philosophies that are relevant to this subject. If I knew more, perhaps I'd show more respect. As it is, so my imaginary critic continues, I have in effect been too narrow-minded, ruling out too swiftly possibilities that merit serious attention.

I certainly agree that we must try and avoid chauvinism. Human beings show far too great a propensity to accept ideas that are in circulation where they happen to have grown up and reject those that are foreign or alien. Indeed, this is one reason to be suspicious of religions, for although religions claim to reveal universal truths about the absolute nature of God, which religion a person believes seems to depend mainly on local contingencies, such as where she was brought up, what religion her parents follow or which exotic religion is currently *en vogue*.

But it would be unfair to single out religion. In philosophy too local biases reign. Philosophers educated in British universities are, on the whole, unsympathetic to much French philosophy, which they see as pretentious, obscurantist and empty. Yet that is not how philosophers educated in France see French philosophy, so clearly local contingencies are having some effect on which kinds of philosophy are seen as good and which as bad.

All this is true. But what follows from it? What cannot follow is that we have to assume all alternative viewpoints are equally valid until we have thoroughly examined them for ourselves and proved otherwise. This is a policy we cannot follow. They are just too many belief systems in the world, too many explanations offered as to why we are here and how we ought to live. How would one set about trying to examine the truth of all of them from within, refusing to be satisfied with what to insiders would seem a superficial understanding? It can't be done because life just isn't long enough. Some of these alternatives actually demand a lifetime of practice, which means you could 'try out' no more than one anyway.

It is impossible to examine a range of belief systems in the kind of depth their followers consider necessary for a real understanding. And yet still it is a common reaction, when someone rejects such a belief system, for people to insist that the refusenik has no right to reject it, because they have not entered into it deeply enough.

This highlights a real dilemma we all face as we try to find meaning and purpose in life. While the virtues of keeping an open mind are widely appreciated, it is not often noted that a certain narrowing of the mind is also required if we are to get anywhere at all. One cannot remain equally open to all possibilities or else one ends up believing nothing. Yet one has to live, one has to make choices about what direction one's life is to take. This is unavoidable. Even to decide not to decide, to conclude that the best way to live life is to maintain a global agnosticism, is to make a decision that one way of life – that of suspension of disbelief – is better than the alternatives.

Given, then, that life is short and decisions about what life means to us cannot be postponed indefinitely, we have to make judgements as best we can without first having gathered all the evidence for and against. This involves some risk, since it is of course possible that we will unjustly neglect an idea which could turn out to be true. But such risks are unavoidable. We risk missing out on good ideas if we spend too much time on a smaller number, thus completely ignoring many others, or if we spend too little time on a great many, thus not doing them full justice.

How, then, can one decide which ideas to devote time to and which to cast aside after relatively little attention? One thing we can do is group ideas together and treat like ideas alike. For example, we may come to the conclusion that we see no reason to believe in God or gods, and we might reach that conclusion after a great deal of thought. Obviously, if a person does this she will probably have focused her thinking around only one or two religions. But if she has concluded, for what she considers to be good reasons, that there is no God, then there is no point in spending a lot of time examining the beliefs of all the religions she knows little about, just as long as those religions maintain belief in God. In other words, you do your long and hard thinking at the most general level possible and don't bother to examine every specific example of the kind of belief you have dismissed.

Another area where this same method is necessary is the subject of the paranormal. There is an inexhaustible supply of claims made about paranormal events. It is literally impossible to assess each one. But you don't need to. If you have examined a range of cases and concluded that there is no evidence for the existence of ghosts or psi-phenomena, then the next time someone says, 'Ah, but how do you explain the tulip-eating poltergeist of old Hampstead Lane?' you simply reply that you don't have to. Experience has shown you that in every other case of alleged hauntings, there has been no actual evidence of the presence of ghosts, and that furthermore all we know about the world and human life suggests there are no such things as ghosts. Hence the onus is not on you to go around looking to disprove every case that you haven't yet come across. Your reasons for disbelieving the stories are good enough and you would be ill advised to continue spending time taking seriously claims you have no reason to accept.

In short, then, one has to develop a kind of hierarchy of beliefs and focus one's attention not on the many specific claims or belief systems which appear to contradict it, but on the most general assumptions themselves. This is why I am not persuaded that I should devote more time to Buddhism, for example. One of the most basic beliefs I have is that human beings are essentially physical animals, and that they cannot survive the death of their brains, at least not unless or until the technology develops to enable the brain to be effectively replicated. This is not a claim I want to defend here. I do, however, think that the evidence that this is true is simply overwhelming, so I have no reason to take seriously any belief system which claims that personality rests on other mysterious forces or principles such as *citta* or *khandhas*. Buddhism is just one example of a general kind of explanation I have become convinced is inadequate and so I do not see the need to examine each example of such a belief system in great detail. In other words, I feel I have to selectively close my mind to these belief systems in order to ensure that my thinking is productive and doesn't just constantly go over old ground.

On the other hand, I do need to keep my mind open when it comes to my overarching commitments. If I see prima facie compelling evidence that I am wrong to hold the strong thesis of human mortality, then the edifice of my beliefs is under threat and I have to look closely at it. But note I need strong prima facie evidence, not just an apparent counter-example or a mere counter-claim. Yet another ghost story or yet another religious creed, invented thousands of years ago when we understood little or nothing about the workings of the brain, is not enough to merit a serious re-examination of my beliefs.

This kind of balancing act is one we all have to do. Your most fundamental beliefs may well be different from mine and accordingly the kinds of claims that you have to ignore or should look at closely will vary. But you have no choice but to implement a similar kind of policy. You cannot and do not go away and thoroughly examine every claim that seems to contradict what you believe. Some you dismiss as just another example of a kind of thinking you reject and some you see as posing an interesting challenge. The key to keeping an open mind is to make these distinctions fairly and honestly, recognizing genuine challenges and always being open to the possibility that a new one might turn up. Most fundamentally, you have to recognize that you may just have got it wrong. But giving equal credence to every alternative is to have not so much an open mind as an empty one.

I am aware that some people may find these later thoughts repugnant. The idea that an open mind is important above all else is so prevalent that any suggestion that some narrowing is essential might be seen as heresy. But it is the only way. Do you treat the claims of Branch Davidians and other fringe Christian cults as seriously as you do the claims of the world's major faiths? When you hear someone has claimed the end of the world is nigh, do you always thoroughly check them out to see if they are right? I hope not. We narrow our minds not just to avoid wasting mental energy but because we have to.

One way in which we do have to keep an open mind, however, is to maintain respect and tolerance for difference. The impossibility of assessing all forms of belief from within should not prevent us from coming down for or against some of them, or from expressing our objections to them clearly and forcefully, as I have done. But it should caution us against ruling out the possibility *tout court* that others may have found a valuable way to live or truths that have eluded us. We are not arrogant to believe what we are sure we have good reasons to believe and reject that which we don't. We are only arrogant if we deny the possibility that we might nevertheless be wrong.

The return of I

To return to the main theme of this chapter, freeing your mind by losing your self does not seem a fruitful path to finding meaning in life. Even if it is true that in one sense the self is an illusion, this gives us no reason to try and dismantle the apparatus that makes the existence of the self possible. Temporarily losing a sense of self also seems to be, ultimately, a way of satisfying the self, and so any technique that delivers this loss of ego has to be judged on whether its effects are a desirable part of a meaningful life. Permanently losing a sense of self is otherwise known as death.

Lessening our attachment to self can help free us from a narcissistic concern for our own well-being and this would be a good thing. But it is at best a means of removing an obstacle to fulfilment, rather than a source of meaning in itself. Certain meditative techniques may help us feel attached to the wider universe, but this doesn't mean we are so attached or that all things are one.

Certainly, there are those who would claim that the kind of enlightenment loss of ego provides cannot be expressed in words, which makes it impossible to analyse in the same way as the other ideas in this book. But I remain convinced that there are no better grounds for assessing ideas than rational arguments. An argument can be clearly stated, assessed and criticized. It doesn't require you to take anything on trust. If it is flawed, it can be shown to be flawed. I am not saying that any idea of any value has to be the product of a rational argument. But I am saying that rational discussion is far and away the best way of examining ideas. The moment someone says that what they think cannot be discussed or debated, then of course there is nothing left to say, or indeed to think about. That's why I make no apology for not discussing or thinking further about any such ideas. That might be thought of as dismissive, but I think it is simply taking the claim that an idea cannot be put into language seriously: there is no point in trying to discuss what cannot be said. You may as well try and drink a symphony.

10

The threat of meaninglessness

My life has no purpose, no direction, no aim, no meaning, and yet I'm happy. I can't figure it out. What am I doing right?
CHARLES SCHULZ, CARTOONIST

The problem with a book on the present king of France is that its subject does not exist. Similarly, the possibility that life is meaningless threatens to make this book, or any discussion on the meaning of life, a discourse on nothing. This threat is real and it reveals itself in various different ways.

In Chapter 8, I introduced the possibility that there just is no meaning and we've got to live with the fact. Charles Schulz, the creator of Snoopy, seems to take this line, but his response is phlegmatic. Albert Camus, on the other hand, thought that the fact – as he saw it – of life's meaninglessness presented one pressing problem: why, then, not kill oneself? Camus thought suicide was not the best option, but that one should confront the 'absurdity' of a meaningless life and live with it, honestly and with courage. Flippantly rejecting the meaningless of life as not presenting a problem, as Schulz did, just wouldn't do. Is life really meaningless, and if so, should we respond like Schulz or like Camus?

Some have a different way of rejecting the idea that life is meaningful. They claim that the so-called problem of meaning is a pseudo-problem. It is not that life is or is not meaningful. It is rather that it makes no sense to talk about life in those terms. It is as futile to ask whether life has meaning as it is to ask whether a piece of music is written in the past or future tense. Life is just not the kind of thing that could have meaning.

The threat of meaningless can manifest itself in a third, rather different way. We might think that though life may have meaning, there is no point in looking for it, since clearly not even the wisest minds in history can agree on what it is and our chances of improving on their efforts are infinitesimally small.

Can these three threats to the possibility of meaning be dispelled?

The meaning of meaningless

Consider first those who deny that life has meaning. The problem here is that often the thought that 'life is meaningless' is only true if we confine oneselves to one narrow way of considering how life could be meaningful. If we do this, we might agree that life is meaningless in those terms. Indeed, this book has effectively done just that. If, for example, we think that for life to have meaning it must have been created with some purpose in mind, then I would agree that life is meaningless *in that sense*. The arguments of Chapter 1 showed, I hope, that we cannot find meaning in the origins of life. If we think that for life to have meaning it must serve some future goal, one which extends beyond this life, then again I would agree that life is meaningless *in that sense*. The arguments of

Chapter 2 were intended to show that life's meaning cannot be indefinitely postponed to some future aim or goal and that, given the evidence for our own mortality, it therefore cannot be located in any purpose beyond or after this life.

It seems to me that when most people say that life is meaningless, they are talking about meaning in one or both of these senses. They are saying – rightly, in my view – that our lives were not created with any purpose or goal in mind and that there is nothing beyond or after life that can provide a purpose for what we do in this life. But to conclude that 'therefore life is meaningless' is simply to ignore the many other ways in which life can be meaningful. When Schulz talked of 'no purpose, no direction, no aim, no meaning' the last item in the list does not have to follow from the first three.

What is missing is the recognition that life can be meaningful if we find it worth living for its own sake, without recourse to further aims, goals or purposes. How that could be so has been the subject of much of this book. Indeed, even Schulz seems to recognize this when he says, 'Yet I'm happy. I can't figure it out. What am I doing right?' What Schulz is pretending he can't understand is that his being content to do what he does is enough to make his life meaningful, since that in itself makes his life worthwhile. His feigned inability to 'figure it out' is simply a product of his assuming that life's meaning has to come from purposes or goals beyond life itself. Once we disabuse ourselves of this notion, there is no puzzle about what Schulz was 'doing right'.

The same kinds of consideration apply when dealing with Camus's question about how we can live life if it is absurd and meaningless. Again it is only 'meaningless' in certain particular senses of the word. It is not that we can remove the problems Camus presents simply by shifting his vocabulary. Of course he realized that in some sense of the word he was himself arguing that one could live meaningfully in a world which was in another sense meaningless. But because he thought recognizing and accepting the 'absurdity' of life were essential for authentic existence, he would have thought that denying life's meaninglessness just because there are different senses of the word 'meaningful' distracts us from confronting the reality of the human situation.

Here we confront a fundamental difficulty. Almost all deniers of meaning in life really seem to be rejecting only the idea that life has a specific kind of meaning: one determined by agents, purposes or principles somehow external to this world. This does not justify the conclusion that life has no meaning at all. Their pronouncement that 'life is meaningless' thus just appears to be a kind of hyperbole.

However, phlegmatic and despondent deniers engage in this hyperbolic discourse for two very different reasons. The phlegmatic deniers are in a sense revelling in the lack of an external source for meaning in life. Schulz can joke about his life having no meaning because, existentially, it doesn't seem to matter. His life is happy and so, in an important sense, meaningful for him. The despondent deniers, on the other hand, think that the lack of such an external source for meaning presents a real difficulty, one that should deeply concern us. To talk about life's meaninglessness is thus considered necessary to bring home the urgency of the situation we face, abandoned to our own devices in a cold, purposeless universe.

Given that these two reactions to the supposed meaninglessness of life – an almost flippant revelling and a po-faced seriousness – are diametrically opposed, it might seem that one or other party has got it seriously wrong. Either Camus needed to lighten up or Schulz should have taken his predicament more seriously. But I'm not sure that either side can be said to have got it right or wrong, because what divides them is not so much their assessment of the facts as how they respond to them emotionally. One can imagine a conversation between the two in which Camus attempts to snap Schulz out of his complacent happiness. Is it not possible that Schulz could agree with everything Camus says about our predicament and yet still turn around at the end of it and say, 'I agree, but that just doesn't bother me as much as it seems to bothers you'?

Those who share Camus's temperament often regard the reactions of those who are more Schulz-like as betraying a kind of shallowness. A certain degree of angst or despair at the purposelessness of the universe is considered a sign that a person has truly grasped the full reality of the human condition. If you're not worried by it, you haven't understood it. But this seems to be no more than a kind of existential snobbery for which ultimately we should blame the romantics. We have this idea that the genius, the poet or the seer has to suffer in some way to truly understand. Wordsworth talked of 'the soothing thoughts that spring / Out of Human suffering'. Proust wrote, 'We are healed from suffering only by experiencing it to the full.' Even the nineteenth-century politician Disraeli was not immune to the romantic bug and said, 'Seeing much, suffering much, and studying much, are the three pillars of learning.' In each case suffering is sanctified as noble and necessary, the price of wisdom.

The problem here is that a general truth has been turned into a cast-iron law. Consider as an analogy the saying 'You learn from your own mistakes.' It would be idiotic to take this to mean that you can learn *only* from your own mistakes. Far better, if possible, to learn from the mistakes of others. As Cato wrote two millennia ago, 'Wise men shun the mistakes of fools.' It is unfortunate that we often don't learn until we make the mistake for ourselves. The important thing is to learn.

In the same way, it is often through suffering that we learn. But it is far better if we can learn without suffering, or learn from the suffering of others (without *making* others suffer, of course). However, some people take the fact that suffering is *often* the route to learning to mean that suffering is somehow *essential* to all learning, or that the person who learns by suffering has necessarily learned more than the person who has learned without suffering. While in general this may be true, it is by no means always true. Many people suffer and never learn. Others learn quickly and avoid the need to suffer altogether.

But perhaps because suffering costs us so much, we feel the need to place a kind of premium on it. We don't like to think that our past suffering was in any way unnecessary or could have been avoided, for that would be to accept that life has been worse than it might otherwise have been for no further benefit. We think those who have suffered less must have missed out on something. It would pain us too much to simply accept that they have been more fortunate than us.

This is, I believe, a kind of bad faith, a failure to accept the role of chance and the purposelessness of much suffering in life. The charge of inauthenticity can thus be turned back on those who, in the spirit of Camus, think that those who phlegmatically accept the purposelessness of the universe lack depth. Those despondent deniers of life's meaningfulness are simply refusing to accept that their own angst is contingent, a reflection of their own temperaments and not an essential form of mental suffering everyone has to go through to live life honestly. The reality is that whether you are phlegmatic or despondent about the purposelessness of the universe depends a great deal on just how you as an individual emotionally respond to it, not on any difference in your depth of understanding.

There may also be social and historical factors at work here. For example, when thinkers like Nietzsche first proclaimed the death of God, it was against a background of a widely shared presupposition that the existence of God was required in order for life to have meaning and for morality to have a basis. Confronted then with the alleged truth that the universe is without purpose, sense or urgency, dislocation and existential panic could be expected. If one assumes the universe does have a purpose, the shattering of that assumption is bound to generate anxiety.

However, if you have grown up without these assumptions, the claim that the universe is devoid of purpose is bound to lose much of its force. If it is not a surprising claim, if it doesn't undermine the basic assumptions that sustain your vision of life and values, then why should you respond to it with anguish and angst? Perhaps, then, the hyperbole of the early existentialists was a product largely of historical factors, reflecting the extent to which their ideas were new, radical, challenging and undermining of the social fabric. We live in a very different world and so should not be surprised if their angst now appears to many of us to be more redolent of adolescence than of genius. *Peanuts* may not be as deep as *The Myth of Sisyphus*, but that doesn't mean Schulz should have been as world-weary as Camus.

Red herrings

The idea that life is meaningless thus seems to be sheer hyperbole. We can accept that the universe is purposeless and that there is no source of meaning outside of this word without concluding that life is itself meaningless.

There is, however, another way of trying to challenge the idea that life must have meaning. That is to claim that life is not the kind of thing that can have meaning, and so the whole idea of 'the meaning of life' is incoherent.

Such an approach is suggested, but not fully articulated, by the logical positivist and ordinary language schools of philosophy that flourished in the early part of the twentieth century in Vienna and Oxford respectively. Both movements are now out of favour, but both were right to claim that philosophical problems can sometimes be the result of the misunderstanding or misuse of language. Sometimes, we can express a problem in perfectly good English which nonetheless masks a deeper incoherence.

Something of the spirit of this is captured by A. J. Ayer's characteristic response to a comment made by the then Bishop of Birmingham, Hugh Montefiore, in a television debate. Ayer had said that meaning could only be given to life by humans. When the bishop objected that, if that were true, life could have no ultimate meaning, Ayer replied, 'I don't know what ultimate meaning means!' Ayer is suggesting that the bishop's words are empty. They appear to be saying something meaningful in English but in fact they mean nothing at all, since no sense can be made of the notion of 'ultimate meaning'.

The argument that 'the meaning of life' is nonsensical is, broadly, that life is not the kind of thing that can be a bearer of meaning, just as a sound cannot be a bearer of colour. So just as 'the colour of a symphony' is literally meaningless (though perhaps metaphorically meaningful) so 'the meaning of life' is literally meaningless (though, again, we may be able to talk of life's meaning in some metaphorical sense).

Consider the various dictionary meanings of 'to mean'. One such meaning is what a thing is intended for. A cake is *meant* to be eaten, because it was created with that intention. But if life is just a product of the natural world, such talk of intention is here inappropriate, for life is not the kind of thing that can be intended for anything.

We can also 'mean' to do something in the sense of intend to do it. So I *meant* to call you, but forgot, for example. But again, life cannot mean in this way, only people can. In the same way, you can say that a person 'means well', but life means neither well nor ill.

'To mean' can also be 'to signify', so that a word 'has a meaning' or a red circular road sign with a thick white horizontal band in the middle 'means' stop. But again, this is not the kind of meaning life can have: life doesn't *signify* anything.

However, the attempt to argue that the whole idea of 'a meaning of life' is incoherent stumbles when it comes to the meaning of 'meaning' which concerns the importance something has, as in 'it means a lot to me'. It is precisely here that life can and does have meaning. It doesn't have meaning in itself, from a neutral perspective. But it means something *to us*. The question 'What is the meaning of life?' may well not fit comfortably with this interpretation, but the question 'How can or does life mean something to us?' certainly does. The question is thus one about why life is of value to us, why we think it to be important and worth living. This is a perfectly coherent question, one which has exercised us in much of this book.

So rather like the debunkers of life's meaning, the deniers that 'the meaning of life' is itself a meaningful notion are guilty of hyperbole. They are right to point out that in some senses of the word it is a kind of nonsense to talk about meaning with respect to life. But life can have meaning in the sense that it is important to us and we value it.

The unexamined life

I think, then, that we can respond to the deniers of 'the meaning of life', all the while accepting that their critiques contain some genuine insights. There is another sceptical response, however. This is to say that, although it can be understood that life does have meaning in some sense of the word, it is pointless to spend your time on earth trying to 'discover' it.

This view can be contrasted with the simple, hedonistic *carpe diem* stance described in Chapter 8, which was a simple and allegedly obvious account of life's meaning. The possibility under consideration now, however, is that the meaning of life is not obvious or transparent but opaque. We can never hope to agree on what the meaning of life is or come up with any final answer. Indeed, there may not be any final answer. Who can tell? So the best policy is just to get on with life and stop worrying about what it means.

Many who are drawn to philosophical reflection themselves find this reaction abhorrent. They are likely to respond by quoting the familiar words of Socrates, 'The unexamined life is not worth living.' We are *Homo quaerens* as well as *Homo sapiens* – creatures that question and reason. If we do not exercise these faculties by living an 'examined life' we are living a less than fully human existence.

One point worth making straight away is that it cannot be assumed that the examined life can be led only by doing philosophy. Socrates preceded his comment on the unexamined life by saying, '. . . daily to discourse about virtue, and of those other things about which you hear me examining myself and others, is the greatest good of man'. This makes it clear that he is praising all forms of rational inquiry. In this sense, there are many ways to examine life, through literature, science, history, or just everyday discussion about people and events. So even if we do wheel out the old Socratic cliché, it doesn't justify the belief that we should all become philosophers of some kind.

Nonetheless, many still do claim that we need to engage in some form of philosophical reflection to make our lives worthwhile. I am suspicious of such a response. It has the whiff of intellectual arrogance about it and perhaps betrays a lack of imagination. People tend to overestimate the importance of the things that interest them the most – for example, the English National Opera, known as ENO, once ran an advertising campaign using a slogan based on its initials: Everyone Needs Opera. What is interesting is not so much that the slogan is patently false, but that it was clearly designed to appeal to opera lovers, and within that group it is not rare to hear people express a similar sentiment. I am reminded of the character in Willy Russell's film *Educating Rita* who exclaimed, 'Wouldn't you just *die* without Mahler?' Well, no, actually, but as an enthusiast she can't help but think of Mahler as being an indispensable part of a full life.

Such special pleading for what interests us is remarkably common. People find it hard to stop at 'I find this really interesting' or 'This is part of what makes life worthwhile for me.' They too often go on to claim, 'Everyone should at least have some knowledge or experience of . . .' whatever it is that moves them. But unless we become full-time dilettantes, trying a week of this and a week of that, they can't all be right.

Of course, at this point the typical advocate of the Socratic injunction to examine one's own life will insist that philosophy is a special case because it is the discipline that underlies all disciplines, the subject that tackles the most fundamental questions. So there really are good reasons for saying that everyone should concern themselves with philosophy, rather than history, poetry, nuclear physics or yoga. I find it hard to disagree, but that doesn't stop me trying. I do think that there are several reasons for thinking that it is not essential to find meaning in life in a philosophically rigorous way.

The first is simply that the majority of people don't ever manage to articulate to themselves a coherent view of what the meaning of life is. The best most people end up with is a kind of motto, a rule of thumb to help them get by from day to day: 'live and let live', 'live for today', 'you reap what you sow', 'call a spade a spade' or 'don't let the buggers get you down'. What is more, most people who go beyond this and embrace a more comprehensive world-view end up with something that is almost certainly false. For example, some embrace Christianity and some Hinduism. Both faiths can't be true, since it is central to one that there is just one God and central to the other that there are many; and reincarnation is essential to one and inconsistent with the other. So at least one – and probably both – are just wrong to think that what they believe will ultimately provide meaning for life (remembering the conclusion of Chapter 3: that religion doesn't actually supply that meaning here and now).

If it is therefore important that we do seek and find some kind of meaning in life, then it seems the vast majority have not lived lives worth living. I know some people are prepared to view humanity as largely a brainless herd out of which only a few noble supermen arise. But I can't join them. To damn the majority of humanity in that way seems to me simply arrogant. Furthermore, as we shall see, such unexamined lives can and do contain many of the ingredients of the life worth living anyway.

Some may say that it is enough to seek meaning and so it doesn't matter if the answers we end up with are wrong. This saves the Christians and the Hindus, who may have got it wrong but have at least examined their own lives. However, it is surely not so easy to divorce the pursuit and that which is pursued. If it is the seeking that counts, it would be better if we all went looking in the wrong direction for the meaning of life than if half of us 'found' it and the other half didn't look at all. But if this is the case, it undermines the importance of the very thing that we are supposed to be searching for. What seems to make the search for meaning important is that this meaning is important. Divorce the thing being pursued from the pursuit and the hunt loses its *raison d'être*.

So if we think that the search for meaning is a kind of ethical imperative, something everyone must engage in to make their lives worthwhile, we seem forced to conclude that most lives are worthless, since people either don't engage in their search or end it with the wrong conclusion. This doesn't prove the falsity of the ethical imperative, but it does show how unpalatable it is.

Fortunately, there is no great mystery about how unexamined or mistaken lives can have meaning. Throughout this book we have seen many ways in which life can have meaning. The overall idea is that life is worth living just as long as it is a good thing in itself. Such a life has meaning because it means something to us, it is valuable to those who have it. Many things can contribute to this: happiness, authenticity and self-expression, social and personal relationships, concern for the welfare of others. All of these things can be part of lives that have not been examined in the systematic way those drawn to philosophizing examine theirs. Hence it is more than possible for someone to live a full and meaningful life without ever having thought in terms of life's meaning.

Some might go further and say that thinking too much about meaning can actually be a barrier to making life meaningful. One has to go on and live life and one cannot do this if one is futilely trying to work out 'what it's all about'. In the words of an advertising slogan that seems to have captured the zeitgeist: just do it. I think this goes too far. Thinking about what life is all about is something many of us can't avoid doing, and the process of thinking it through can, I believe, help us identify mistaken ways of thinking about life and identify more fruitful ones, even if there is no final answer. That is what I hope reading this book will help people to do. I do not agree that we *should* cease thinking about the meaning of life altogether. Nevertheless, I do agree that we can only think about it so much and I also agree that for people who just don't have the inquiring impulse, life can be meaningful in the absence of any such questioning.

For those still impressed by the need to examine life as much as possible, consider the question of having children. Few things make more difference to the direction of one's life than the decision to start a family. And yet how often is this a conscious decision, based on a process that involves thoroughly going through the options and concluding with clarity and a fair degree of certainty that this is the right choice for both parents? More often than not, I would suggest, this most important of all life choices is made not on the basis of a Socratic inquiry into the nature and purpose of life. Despite all we might say about the need to think about life's meaning and take control of our destinies, having children is still something that we end up doing or not doing for reasons that are far from clear to us.

Again, it might be said that all this shows is just how unreflective much of humanity is. However, I think what it shows is that when it comes to the vital choices we make, the ones that form our lives, a good deal will always pass relatively unexamined. We delude ourselves if we think that we can more or less fully direct our lives by analysing what it's all about and behaving accordingly. This is the truth dimly perceived by those who argue that we should forget about the meaning of life and just get on with it. Their conclusion is too extreme, but their argument is based on insights that puncture the pretensions of those who think life can and should be planned according to a fully thought-out picture of what it is all about.

I may have been guilty of playing devil's advocate here and overstating my case. If I have done so, it is in order to dispel any impression I might otherwise give that my subject, philosophy, should be your subject too. I do, nonetheless, think that for most people some philosophizing is unavoidable. We do it whether we recognize it as philosophy or not. Every time we think about what the right thing to do is, what the truth is or what it means to be a person, we are beginning to do philosophy. So for the vast majority, philosophy does enter into our lives, does help us to examine them and does help us to gain a clearer idea of what life is all about. If I have underplayed this it is only because I do not think it follows from this that everyone should read much more philosophy (though it would be good if more philosophy were read) or go and join some kind of philosophy discussion group (these are sometimes little more than exchanges of opinions among opinionated windbags). I believe as a society we would benefit from being more philosophical, but I'm not convinced we need more philosophers. And if you've spent much time around them, you might agree.

11

Of which reason knows nothing

The man who listens to Reason is lost: Reason enslaves all whose minds are not strong enough to master her.

GEORGE BERNARD SHAW, *MAN AND SUPERMAN*

The account I have offered so far could be fairly described as rationalist and humanist. It is rationalist in the sense that it is guided by reasoned argument and not by intuition, revelation, appeals to authority or superstition. It is humanistic in that it claims human life contains the source and measure of its own value.

This kind of rationalist-humanistic approach leaves many unsatisfied. On the one hand, it can appear to be hubristic, granting too much to human choice and desire and failing to recognize that human standards and values can never be enough. On the other hand, it can seem insufficiently ambitious, apparently disregarding the non-rational side of human life. We sometimes have to abandon reason if we are to fully embrace life. It is no coincidence that the characters in many love songs are described as fools. As the French philosopher Blaise Pascal wrote, 'The heart has its reasons of which reason knows nothing.'

These criticisms, though motivated by legitimate concerns, are misplaced. They caricature humanists as sterile, unfeeling rationalists with no sensitivity to the emotional side of life or to the limits of human understanding. The reality, as I hope to show, is that rational humanism can and should be sensitively attuned to the emotional, moral and mysterious.

Meaningful evil

Consider first the criticism that the standards and measures internal to human life are never enough to give it value and meaning. One example of this general kind of objection is described by John Cottingham in his book *On the Meaning of Life*. Cottingham argues that we cannot separate the question of the morality of a life from the question of its meaning, and that moral measure (and so also meaning's measure) must come from an 'overarching structure or theory' rooted outside of our purely human interests for it to be real. If not, he fears, any 'engaged life in which the agent is systematically committed to certain projects he makes his own' is meaningful, 'irrespective of [its] moral status'.

The criticism echoes a popular objection to Sartrean notions of authenticity. The problem, objectors claim, is that existentialists like Sartre argue that we need to create meaning and purpose for ourselves, but they do not provide any guidance on what kinds of choices are morally acceptable. It is conceivable, for example, that someone might find meaning and purpose by joining the Gestapo. But can we really say that such a life, dedicated as it is to persecuting others, would be meaningful?

Although I have drawn on Sartre in this book, I have not claimed that authenticity is the only or even the most important virtue which gives life meaning. (Nor am I convinced Sartre did, for that matter.) Nevertheless, following Cottingham, it might be argued that because my account depends upon our determining what makes life worth living *for us*, it has effectively cut morality adrift from genuine standards in a similar way. The reason for this is that I have defined (in shorthand, anyway) a meaningful life as one that is meaningful or has value *for us*, and it is always possible that someone may choose a life which is meaningful *for her* but which is thoroughly immoral.

There are two possible responses to this. Consider the question of whether it is true that a meaningful life has to be a moral one. We could simply reject this. Why not just say that meaning and morality are separate? That does not and cannot mean that it is 'OK' for someone to live a meaningful but immoral life, since, if morality is separate from meaning, there is nothing good or bad in itself about living a meaningful life. Because we are used to thinking of meaning and morality in life as being linked, it may sound odd to say that the Gestapo officer can have a meaningful but immoral life. However, there is nothing contradictory or ethically objectionable about doing so.

The second response is to say that this does violence to the concept of a meaningful life and we must accept that meaning and morality are connected. That too can be accommodated in my position. I have argued that a meaningful life has to have value for us, but if it is also true that a meaningful life has to be moral, all we have to do is add that as a condition of a meaningful life. To put it quasi-technically, it is a necessary condition of a life being meaningful that it is of value to the person living the life, but that is not by itself a sufficient condition. The life also needs to be a moral one. Hence the necessary and sufficient conditions of a meaningful life are that it is of value to the person living it *and* it is morally good.

Whether we take the first or second route is not terribly important. It depends solely on whether we think the concepts of meaning and morality in life can be separated. If we think they can, we should take the first route and say that there are no grounds for saying that there is anything good about an immoral life which has meaning. If we think they cannot be divorced, we take the second route and say that a life which seems of value to the person living it is nonetheless not meaningful if it is an immoral one.

It could be objected that this second route avoids the objection merely by adding an ad hoc condition that a meaningful life has to be moral, which is not necessitated by the account I have offered. Rather, it has simply been grafted on to solve an awkward problem. I think this charge can be rejected, because morality does have a vital place in my account. I have argued that the only thing that can make life meaningful is the recognition that human life is worth living in itself. To recognize this is to recognize something that is true of all human (and perhaps some animal) life. This means accepting that each of us has an equal claim to the good things in life, and that making a person's life worse than it need be is a moral wrong.

Furthermore, I have so far been a little generous with my imagined critics, because I have overstated the extent to which the assessment of meaning is a purely individual affair. In fact, the constant in my account has been that life has to have value in itself and that value has to be for the person living the life. But that does not necessarily mean that the only person able to judge the value is the person living the life, or indeed that they have to consciously recognize its value at all. This is why I allowed in Chapter 10 for the possibility that the unexamined life could be worth living. It is also perfectly compatible with the account I have given to say that we may be mistaken or ignorant about the value and meaning of our own lives. So it does not simply follow from the fact that a person *thinks* they have a meaningful life that they actually do.

Much more could be said both for and against the idea that my account provides the required room for morality. What I hope to have shown, however, is simply that it is not true that the position I have defended leaves us unable to criticize anyone who chooses a life for themselves which is morally abhorrent. I have not argued that individual choice is the be-all and end-all. It is simply a caricature of humanistic philosophy to say that it makes individual men and women the incontestable measure of all things.

Maintaining mystery

A second type of argument against the kind of humanistic account I have offered again levels the charge of hubris. This time the objection is that my way of 'demystifying' goes too far. What I have attempted to do is bring everything within the scope of human understanding and reject anything that might be in some sense beyond comprehension. What I should do, however, is accept that there is much more to life than that which can be understood by mere mortals and that living a meaningful life requires us to be attuned to the mysterious, unexplained features of reality.

In some respects, this objection is no more than a plea on behalf of those who don't like the idea that the meaning of life can be demystified and is in some sense quite humdrum. It is all very well complaining that my account leaves no room for mystery, but if it leaves nothing mysterious perhaps the right conclusion to draw is that there is no mystery left.

But it is also simply false that my account leaves no room at all for mystery. One reason for this is that there is nothing essentially dogmatic about the position I have argued for. I have not said, for example, that there is no way there could be a transcendental realm. All I have argued is that, in the absence of good reasons to think there is, to believe requires the risk of faith. Nor have I denied that certain religious forms of life might be capable of providing people with value in life. I have simply argued that it is legitimate for me to reject them for reasons I think hold good for others too.

Most importantly, the account I have offered is more of a framework than a prescription, and when it comes to filling in the details, there is a great deal of mystery to please those who do not like life to be too clear-cut. The main source of this mystery is not some transcendental reality but human nature itself. The fact is that we human beings are much too complex and surprising for any sensible person to be able to say that life holds no mystery.

Actually constructing meaningful lives for ourselves requires us to confront all sorts of mysteries not explained by this book. These are mysteries of what makes us tick, what we discover is most important to us, what we learn about our own desires that we never knew, what we do that we thought we were never capable of doing. There is no danger of our confronting a future without mystery and surprise, because life twists and turns unexpectedly and we often remain mysteries to ourselves.

There is another kind of attunement to mystery which I think is valuable and which can easily be neglected if we focus too much on what we have to do to find meaning for ourselves. This is the feeling which in religious terms would be called gratitude or thankfulness. This is not merely the thought that we are lucky to be alive (if we are lucky to be alive) but that we owe this fact to something other than ourselves. Religious forms of life ritualize appreciation for this fact, in daily prayers and grace before meals, for example. Those who do not believe in any God to direct such thanks towards do not have the same motivation to meditate regularly on the contingency of their existence and its dependence on forces beyond their control.

It does not require a belief in God to feel thankful to be alive, or to appreciate that not everything in life is for us to determine. Both ways of thinking are, I believe, valuable. They promote a proper appreciation of life and due humility. Reminding ourselves that we are fortunate to have the meals we eat, the friends we have, those members of our families with whom we truly do have bonds, and so on, helps maintain a sense of perspective which makes appreciating life easier. Those whose religious practices already include reminders of such things therefore do something valuable from which non-believers can learn.

This, however, is very different from the kinds of cherished, imprecise beliefs that people often seem to be thinking of when they talk about respect for mystery. What many think of as mystery is often more a vague sense that there must be a God or an afterlife; that they are more than just mortal human beings; and that morality is a part of objective reality and not the human world. And what motivates the desire to protect this kind of mystery is, I think, often a kind of fear: a fear that if we cannot depend on there being a God, an afterlife, a soul and values other than those we hold, then we have to take responsibility for making what we can of what is probably the only life we have.

If we have such a fear then we need to confront and defeat it. For whether there is a life to come or not, this life is of value in itself and is the only one we are in a position to change. And we cannot avoid having to work out for ourselves where the value in this life lies. This does not make us gods, for we can choose well or badly. The majority of those who think that mere pleasure or worldly success will provide them with full lives, for example, are just wrong. So we face choices and shoulder responsibilities. We can succeed as well as fail.

All you need is love?

The recognition of the fragility of human life and all in it, as well as the ever-present possibility of tragedy, is essential to understanding the role of love in the meaningful life. Love in its various forms is clearly of vital importance to human beings and is one of the things that makes existence worthwhile. One reason why I have not said more about it so far is that it is an area of life where we can perhaps obtain more guidance from novels, plays, films and poems than we can from systematic philosophy. It might be significant that there is relatively little in the great works of philosophy about love and that many of the most important contemporary philosophers to write on the subject, such as Martha Nussbaum and Raimond Gaita, do so through discussions of literature.

Nevertheless, love runs as a kind of invisible thread through all the main discussions of this book. In every case, love exemplifies the importance and limits of seeing life's meaning in terms of the possibilities I have set out.

Consider the injunction to do good. Altruism cannot be motivated by pure reason alone. Rationality by itself is not directed at any good for humans or anything else. This is what Hume meant when he wrote, ''Tis not contrary to reason to prefer the destruction of the whole world to the scratching of my finger.' The desire to do good is rooted not in reason but in the varieties of love: the love for a partner, familial love or a kind of general love or fellow feeling for others. Without such love, all the rational reasons in the world would not be enough to motivate us to do good. As Hume put it in another memorable phrase, 'Reason is, and ought to be, only the slave of the passions.' Hume is a philosophical hero for many rationalist-humanists. So much for the elevation of reason above feeling.

This also explains why the desire to serve humanity is misplaced. The species is an abstraction and as such is not an appropriate recipient of our love. We should reserve that for sentient creatures who can respond to it.

Love also sheds light on our desire for happiness. The desire for love is connected with the desire for happiness. But no one who truly loves can in good faith reduce love to the pursuit of happiness. Love is much more bittersweet than that. True love, be it romantic, familial or platonic, persists through unhappiness and has as its subject the welfare of the persons loved, not the lover. Love, then, reflects the important role of happiness in the meaningful life, but also the shallowness of seeing happiness as all.

We want to love and to be loved for who we are, which illustrates the value we place on authenticity. At the same time, the kind of openness this demands can be very threatening and leave us feeling vulnerable. It is therefore very easy to succumb to bad faith, hiding from truths about ourselves and others that would make love more difficult or threaten its survival. The demands and difficulties of living authentically are nowhere more evident than in our close relationships with others.

Considering success in love also provides an insight into the nature of genuine success. A relationship is never successful in the sense of achieving a desired outcome. Success in love is an ongoing project and is always precarious. In this way, it perfectly exemplifies the kind of true success I argued could contribute to a meaningful life.

Love also requires us sometimes to seize the day. Because love is valuable and opportunities to find it relatively rare, we are fools to let chances for real love pass us by or delay reconciliation with estranged friends or family we still have strong feelings for. Of course, this line of reasoning has been used as a mere seduction technique, from the eloquent lines of Andrew Marvell's metaphysical poems to the clumsy chat-up lines uttered in bars and clubs. But the line is only effective because it reflects a truth that haunts us: too much caution, and love can pass us by.

One reason why the unexamined life can still be worth living is that it can be a life full of love. You don't need to engage in philosophical reflection to have strong emotional attachments. The world's most famous rock and roll casualty, Ozzy Osbourne, would be the first to admit that he is no philosopher. 'I've been known to do some pretty nutty shit,' he testified with his trademark bluntness. 'There's no doubt about it – I am fucking nuts.' But Sharon, a woman for whom the phrase 'long-suffering wife' could have been invented, gives him a reason to fight his demons and addictions and live. 'I love this woman more than anything in the world,' he says. 'I would not survive without her.'

Philosophy is best suited to examining what is rational, within our control, the object of choice and closely analysable. Love is, if not irrational, then at least not driven by rationality. It is not entirely out of our control, but nor is it by any means fully under our command. We can to some extent choose what we do when we love, but we cannot choose what or who we love. And love is best described not in the language of forensic philosophy, but in literature, poetry and song.

It is not, then, true that love shows the rationalist-humanist approach to be misguided. Rather, it exemplifies the limits of human powers to understand and master life, which any adequate humanist account of the meaning of existence must accept. But it also shows something profound to which humanism can make claim. Love is not immortal or invincible. Sadly, it is not true that all you need is love. Love, like life, is valuable, but fragile and subject to no guarantees. It is fraught with risk and disappointment, as well as being the source of great elation and joy.

The humanist, who sees this life as providing the only available source of meaning, accepts all this, just as she accepts the claims of morality without transcendental support and the existence of mystery without seeing it as a place-holder for the divine. The transcendentalist, in contrast, wants what is of value in life to be underwritten by a high order. Love isn't good enough unless it is all-conquering and can triumph even over death. Morality is not morality if it is rooted only in human life. Mystery is intolerable if it merely reflects the limits of human understanding. The transcendentalist's desire for something more is understandable, but the humanist's refusal to succumb is, I believe, a sign of her ability to confront and accept the limits of human understanding and, ultimately, human existence.

Conclusion

Well, that's the end of the film. Now, here's the meaning of life. (An envelope is handed to her. She opens it in a businesslike way.) Thank you, Brigitte. (She reads.) . . . Well, it's nothing very special. Try and be nice to people, avoid eating fat, read a good book every now and then, get some walking in, and try and live together in peace and harmony with people of all creeds and nations.
MONTY PYTHON'S THE MEANING OF LIFE

The meaning of life may not be quite as simple as the end of the Monty Python film suggests, but if the arguments I have offered are correct, the movie is not far off the mark. As I said in the introduction, this book has offered, not a big secret, but a deflationary account of life's meaning, reducing the vague, mysterious question of the meaning of life to a series of more specific and thoroughly unmysterious questions about what gives life purpose and value. To understand life's meaning therefore does not require rare wisdom.

Like the conclusion of the Monty Python film, in one sense the account I have offered is 'nothing very special'. But the simplicity of the conclusion should not detract from its significance. The mere fact that life's meaning is available and potentially evident to all is a major challenge to those who see themselves as the guardians of life's significance: the priests, gurus and teachers who would have us think life's meaning is beyond ordinary mortals. To challenge this view is to challenge the power others seek to exert over us by their claims to special knowledge. The main argument of this book is therefore democratic and egalitarian, in that it returns to each of us the power and responsibility to discover and in part determine meaning for ourselves.

The simplicity of the conclusion is also deceptive because what is simple is not always easy or obvious. It is straightforward enough to say that life can be worthwhile in itself, particularly if it is a life with a balance of authenticity, happiness and concern for others; one where time is not wasted; one which engages in the ongoing work of becoming who we want to be and being successful in those terms. But putting this all into practice is difficult. Indeed, it carries with it a risk we saw when looking at success, namely that we will set ourselves an unrealistically high standard and end up being dissatisfied with life as a result. The sobering truth is that life involves ongoing struggle. One can understand what the elements of a meaningful life are, but they do not provide a simple recipe for contentment and satisfaction.

This is part of the reason why I feel a little uneasy finishing this book. Writers no longer complete books by sitting at their typewriters and punching out 'The End' triumphantly. Today, the end is marked by clicking the computer mouse to save and close for what one decides is the last time. Yet with a subject like the meaning of life, how can one ever feel that one has said enough or covered everything? Like the tourists who spend a weekend in Rome and say they've 'done' the eternal city, there would be something suspect about writing this book and concluding I had 'done' the meaning of life.

The obvious truth at the source of this unease is that there is no last word on this subject. The ambitions of this book, which are in some ways modest and in other ways immodest, have been to articulate the general philosophical considerations which bring clarity to the question of life's meaning. This leaves us with a kind of framework, one which is provisional and may be adapted, but more significantly one which can be fleshed out and made real in more ways than are imaginable by any one mind. In adding these details, in actually trying to live a meaningful life, we need to look to psychologists, novelists, artists and poets as well as philosophers. Philosophy has a valuable contribution to make, but to live life meaningfully, we need to be more than philosophers. As David Hume said, 'Be a philosopher; but, amidst all your philosophy, be still a man.'

One further reason why no book can provide the last word on life's meaning is that we are each of us different and when we set about living our own particular lives we have to make many choices that only we can make. We have the same needs as other people – for friendship, food, pleasure, happiness, success and so forth – but these needs vary greatly in their nature and intensity from person to person. For instance, some people can barely stand being alone for an hour, others love solitude. Some are thrill seekers, genuinely needing bursts of intense experience, while others prefer quieter lives and find such intensities distracting. Some like to live the life of the mind, some live to feel the pulsating beats of dance music, while others feel both needs strongly. For that reason any 'guide to the meaning of life' cannot be a complete instruction manual but can only establish the framework within which each individual can construct a worthwhile life.

To do so, however, means confronting the fragility, unpredictability and contingency of life and doing the best we can with it. This should be a source of hope rather than despair. If the meaning of life is not a mystery, if leading meaningful lives is within the power of us all, then we do not need to ask the question 'What's it all about?' in despair. We can look around us and see the many ways in which life can be meaningful. We can see the value of happiness while accepting that it is not everything, which will make it easier for us at those times when it eludes us. We can learn to appreciate the pleasures of life without becoming slaves to appetites which can never be satisfied. We can see the value of success, while not interpreting that too narrowly, so that we can appreciate the project of striving to become what we want to be as well as the more visible, public signs of success. We can see the value of seizing the day, without that leading us into a desperate scramble to grasp the ungraspable moment. We can appreciate the value in helping others lead meaningful lives, too, without thinking that altruism demands everything we have. And finally, we can recognize the value of love, as perhaps the most powerful motivator to do anything at all.

Further reading and references

Introduction

You can also learn much which is true and wise in Douglas Adams's *Hitch Hiker's Guide to the Galaxy* books (Pan).

1 Looking for the blueprint

For more – but not too much more – on why the traditional arguments for the existence of God fail, see the philosophy of religion chapter in my *Philosophy: Key Themes* (Palgrave Macmillan). An even brisker run through them is in my *Atheism: A Very Short Introduction* (Oxford University Press).

Two useful web resources used were the *Online Etymology Dictionary* www.etymonline.com and the PBS's history of the Big Bang for beginners www.pbs.org/deepspace/timeline.

Mary Shelley's *Frankenstein* is available in many editions, including the one I used from Oxford University Press.

Aristotle's discussion of causation comes in his *Metaphysics* (Penguin).

The Bertrand Russell quotes are from his *Sceptical Essays* (Routledge).

I refer to and strongly recommend Richard Dawkins's *The Selfish Gene* (Oxford University Press) in order to properly understand evolution.

Three key existentialist texts that are the source of several references are *The Will to Power* by Friedrich Nietzsche (Penguin), *Existentialism and*

Humanism by Jean-Paul Sartre (Methuen) and *The Myth of Sisyphus* by Albert Camus (Penguin).

The Daniel Dennett quote is from an interview at http://www.pbs.org/saf/1103/hotline/hdennett.htm.

Eugene Cernan's quote comes from the *Observer* magazine, 16 June 2002.

The genetic fallacy was first described by Morris R. Cohen and Ernest Nagel in *An Introduction to Logic and Scientific Method* (Simon Paperbacks).

2 Living life forwards

The Hobbes references are from his *Leviathan* (Penguin).

Aristotle's *Nicomachean Ethics*, better known as simply *Ethics* (Penguin), is still a remarkable source of insight into how to live well.

Peter Singer's *How are We to Live?* (Oxford University Press) is well worth a read. The anecdote about the Dallas Cowboys coach he mentions comes from Alfie Kohn's *No Contest* (Houghton Mifflin).

Kierkegaard's various spheres or stages of existence are discussed in the interminable *Either/Or* (Penguin) and the more manageable *Stages on Life's Way* (Princeton University Press), while he discusses the religious motivation for his thought in *The Point of View* (Princeton University Press).

Hegel's dialectical method is described in *The Phenomenology of Spirit* (Oxford University Press). Again, this is a large and difficult work, so you might prefer Peter Singer's primer *Hegel: A Very Short Introduction* (Oxford University Press).

Philip Larkin's 'Next, Please' is in his *Collected Poems* (Faber).

The Marcus Aurelius quote comes from his *Meditations* (Penguin).

Oliver James's *Britain on the Couch* (Century) will crop up again in Chapter 6.

Although the business card incident in the film *American Psycho* doesn't appear exactly as described in the source novel, Bret Easton Ellis's vicious satire (Picador) covers the same theme brilliantly, if you can cope with some truly appalling sadistic violence.

Sartre discusses bad faith in *Being and Nothingness* (Routledge). It's a long and difficult book, and a better introduction to Sartre's thought might be *Jean-Paul Sartre: Basic Writings*, ed. Stephen Priest (Routledge). This volume includes *Existentialism and Humanism*, mentioned in Chapter 1.

Hope Edelman is quoted from *The Bitch in the House: 26 Women Tell the Truth About Sex, Solitude, Work, Motherhood and Marriage*, ed. Cathi Hanauer (Viking). It came to my attention via Joan Smith's review in the *Observer*, 23 March 2003.

3 More things in heaven and earth

The Lukas Moodysson interview was in the *Observer*, 13 April 2003.

The Bertrand Russell quote is from *Why I am Not a Christian* (Routledge) and is a good example of a book that will please atheists but won't persuade the religious.

Spinoza's pantheistic philosophy is spelled out in his *Ethics* (Hackett).

Kierkegaard's *Fear and Trembling* (Penguin) is a classic study of faith, of interest to everyone.

Space would not allow me to say more about the philosophy of personal identity, which was the topic of my own PhD. I strongly recommend *Personal Identity*, ed. John Perry (University of California Press) and *I: The*

Philosophy and Psychology of Personal Identity by Jonathan Glover (Penguin) for anyone interested in the topic.

Albert Camus's contribution to this chapter comes from *The Plague* (Penguin), while Sartre we've met in previous chapters.

Bernard Williams's 'The Makropulos Case' is in *Problems of the Self* (Cambridge University Press).

4 Here to help

The Norwegian couple and the Jewish child are discussed in Philippa Foot's perceptive *Natural Goodness* (Oxford University Press), which is one of those books you can learn a lot from even when you disagree with it, as I do.

The examples of phrases used in volunteer advertisements all came from page 41 of *The Big Issue*, 9–15 June 2003, one of the most important places for volunteer ads in London.

The core text for Kant's moral philosophy is *The Groundwork of the Metaphysics of Morals* (Cambridge University Press), the ideas of which are taken further in the inventively named sequel, *The Metaphysics of Morals* (Cambridge University Press).

The Bertrand Russell quote comes from his *The Problems of Philosophy* (Oxford University Press).

The happiness survey was conducted by Mintel and quoted in the *Observer* magazine, 15 June 2003.

Diderot's line about the solitary is in his play *The Natural Son*. It is chiefly remembered because Rousseau, in his *Confessions* (Wordsworth), cites the line, believing it to be directed against him.

5 The greater good

The Margaret Thatcher quote is from an article, 'Aids, Education and the Year 2000', in *Woman's Own*, 3 October 1987.

Derek Parfit's *Reasons and Persons* (Oxford University Press) is a classic, and much more interesting than the small section I refer to here suggests.

Richard Dawkins's *The Selfish Gene* (Oxford University Press) was first mentioned in Chapter 1.

Jonathan Glover's *Humanity: A Moral History of the Twentieth Century* (Pimlico) is, among many other things, an instructive warning against placing abstract or ideological goods over human welfare, as is George Orwell's *Animal Farm* (Penguin).

David Cooper argues that raw humanism is unliveable in his erudite and wide-ranging *The Measure of Things: Humanism, Humility and Mystery* (Oxford University Press).

6 As long as you're happy

Schopenhauer's thoughts on pleasure and happiness are to be found in his *Essays and Aphorisms* (Penguin). Aristotle's discussion of the same themes is in his *Ethics* (Penguin), while those of Epicurus can be found in *The Epicurean Philosophers*, ed. John Gaskin (Everyman), and those of Mill in *Utilitarianism*, collected in *On Liberty and Other Essays* (Oxford University Press).

The Kant quote comes from *The Groundwork of the Metaphysics of Morals* (Cambridge University Press).

Jane Goodall's *In the Shadow of Man* (Weidenfeld & Nicolson) gives a fascinating account of her life with chimpanzees.

For a challenge to the ratiocentric bias of modern western philosophy, see John Cottingham's excellent *Philosophy and the Good Life* (Cambridge University Press).

Robert Nozick's famous experience machine thought experiment is in *Anarchy, State and Utopia* (Blackwell).

Aldous Huxley's *Brave New World* is published by Flamingo.

Oliver James confronts the question of why we are getting richer but no happier in *Britain on the Couch* (Century).

The George Bernard Shaw quote comes from *Man and Superman* (Penguin).

An excellent account of the Stoic philosophers and much more besides is to be found in Anthony Gottlieb's *The Dream of Reason: A History of Philosophy from the Greeks to the Renaissance* (Penguin).

The trial of Socrates is described in Plato's *Apology*, anthologized in *The Last Days of Socrates* (Penguin).

7 Becoming a contender

Sartre's *Existentialism and Humanism* crops up again (see Chapter 2).

The text of Chekhov's *The Seagull* I used is at the *Online Library and Digital Archive* at http://ibiblio.org.

Gilbert Ryle's thoughts on counterfeit coins are in 'Perception', in *Dilemmas* (Cambridge University Press).

Jonathan Rée talks about 'becoming a philosopher' in the introduction to *The Kierkegaard Reader*, ed. Rée and Jane Chamberlain (Blackwell), and also in the introductory notes to 'Johannes Climacus'. Kierkegaard is worth your time and this volume is a good place to start.

For the free will debate, David Hume discusses his compatibilism in *An Enquiry Concerning Human Understanding* (Oxford University Press) and A. J. Ayer takes up the baton in the twentieth century in his *Philosophical Essays* (Macmillan). Kant talks about the necessity of postulating free will in his *Groundwork of the Metaphysics of Morals* (Cambridge University Press). Ted Honderich rejects compatibilism in his accessible but original *How Free are You?* (Oxford University Press). If you want to get up to date with the latest, often complicated, thinking on the subject, *Free Will*, ed. Robert Kane (Blackwell), contains plenty of challenging homework.

The Epicurean Philosophers, ed. John Gaskin (Everyman), requires another mention.

8 Carpe diem

Horace seizes the day in his *Complete Odes and Epodes* (Oxford University Press).

The Kate Bush song 'Moments of Pleasure' is from *The Red Shoes* (EMI) and the Rush ditty 'Time Stand Still' from *Hold Your Fire* (Vertigo).

Kierkegaard's *Stages on Life's Way* (Princeton University Press) and *Either/Or* (Penguin) are again important sources here.

Hannay's discussion of Kierkegaard is in his *Kierkegaard* (Routledge).

The idea of the systematic elusiveness of 'now' is a corruption of Gilbert Ryle's systematic elusiveness of 'I' in *The Concept of Mind* (Penguin).

Galen Strawson's paper 'The Self' is collected in *Personal Identity*, ed. by Raymond Martin and John Barresi (Penguin). Another paper more specifically about episodics and diachronics, probably to be called 'Against Narrativity', will be published in 2005 in *The Self*, ed. Strawson (Blackwell).

Dorothy Parker's poem 'The Flaw in Paganism' is in *The Best of Dorothy Parker* (Duckworth).

Plato talks about pleasure in *Philebus* (Penguin), while Aristotle's *Ethics* (Penguin) again merits attention.

If you don't know the Sartre source now, you never will.

The Colin Farrell quote comes from the *Toronto Star*, 5 April 2003.

Are You Experienced? by William Sutcliffe is published by Penguin.

9 Lose your self

Descartes thought he was in his *Discourse on Method*, available in one volume with his *Meditations* (Penguin).

Hume's 'bundle theory' of the self is in *A Treatise of Human Nature*, Book One (Oxford University Press).

The Sister Vajira verses are cited in 'No Inner Core – Anattá' by Sayadaw U Silananda, at www.buddhistinformation.com/no_inner_core.htm. A good introduction to Buddhism is *Buddhism: A Very Short Introduction* by Damien Keown (Oxford University Press).

Russell warns of the feverish and confined life at the end of *The Problems of Philosophy* (Oxford University Press).

Nietzsche talks about life-denying 'slave morality' in his classic *On the Genealogy of Morals* (Oxford University Press).

The Madonna quote comes from the *Observer*, 8 June 2003.

Wittgenstein tells us to be silent about what we can't speak about in his *Tractatus Logico-Philosophicus* (Routledge).

David Cooper makes as much sense of the ineffable as is possible in *The Measure of Things* (Oxford University Press).

10 The threat of meaninglessness

Camus talks about the absurd in *The Myth of Sisyphus* (Penguin).

A. J. Ayer's *Language, Truth and Logic* (Penguin) is the classic exposition of his logical positivism, although the quote I cite is from an article, 'Universal Truths', by Paul Davies in the *Guardian*, 23 January 2003. Logical positivism is now a dead duck, but there are many valuable insights in the ordinary language school of philosophy. See J. L. Austin's *Philosophical Papers* (Clarendon) for some of them.

The 'unexamined life' line comes from Plato's *Apology*, in *The Last Days of Socrates* (Penguin).

Nicholas Rescher calls us *Homo quaerens* in his *Philosophical Reasoning* (Blackwell), which has little to do with the themes of this book but is well worth reading nonetheless.

If it's all getting too heavy, homespun philosophy is always available at the Official Peanuts Website www.unitedmedia.com/comics/peanuts.

11 Of which reason knows nothing

If you read only one book on what I refer to as rationalist-humanism, make it Richard Norman's *On Humanism* (Routledge).

The Pascal quote is from his *Pensées* (Penguin).

John Cottingham's *On the Meaning of Life* (Routledge) is a kind of preemptive objection to much of this book and is worth reading, especially for those whom I have failed to convince that we don't need to rely on the spiritual for meaning.

David Cooper gives a much deeper analysis of the value of mystery than I do justice to here in his *The Measure of Things* (Oxford University Press).

Hume talks of finger-scratching in his *A Treatise of Human Nature* (Oxford University Press).

Ozzy Osbourne is quoted from an interview by Paul Elliott in *Mojo*, November 2003.

Conclusion

The Hume quote is from *An Enquiry Concerning Human Understanding* (Oxford University Press).

Finally, for all remaining unanswered questions, please refer to *Monty Python's The Meaning of Life*, book of the film (Methuen).

Index

Credits

'The Flaw in Paganism' by Dorothy Parker, used by permission of Gerald Duckworth & Co Ltd.

'Free Your Mind and Your Ass Will Follow' written by George Clinton, Jr./Luscious Ross/Eddie Hazel, used by permission of Publisher: Bridgeport Music Inc. (BMI) and Southfield Music Inc. (ASCAP).

Quotation from *Man and Superman* by George Bernard Shaw, used by permission of The Society of Authors, on behalf of the Bernard Shaw Estate.

'Moments of Pleasure' words and music by Kate Bush © 1993, reproduced by permission of Kate Bush trading as Noble & Brite, London WC2H 0QY.

Quotation from 'Next Please' by Philip Larkin, reprinted from *The Less Deceived* by permission of The Marvell Press, England and Australia.

Quotation from *Secrets of Closing the Sale* by Zig Ziglar, used by permission of Revell, a division of Baker Publishing Group, © 2004 (revised edition).

While every effort has been made to trace copyright holders of quoted text, this has in some cases proved impossible. The publisher is prepared to make suitable acknowledgement in any reissue or reprint of the work.